HUMANIZING
THE CLASSROOM

HUMANIZING THE CLASSROOM

Models of Teaching in Affective Education

JOHN P. MILLER

Ontario Institute for Studies in Education, Northwestern Centre

97334

Praeger Publishers
New York

Published in the United States of America in 1976
by Praeger Publishers, Inc.
111 Fourth Avenue, New York, N.Y. 10003

Library of Congress Cataloging in Publication Data

Miller, John P.
  Humanizing the Classroom.

  Bibliography: p.
  Includes index.
  1. Learning, Psychology of. 2. Group relations training. I. Title
LB1051.M493   371.1'02   75–40280
ISBN 0–275–49940–5
ISBN 0–275–64330–1 pbk.

Printed in the United States of America

PREFACE

Values clarification, psychosynthesis, synectics, confluent education, psychological education, human relations training—the list
of recent teaching approaches in affective education is long and
varied. Although these approaches offer many alternatives to
teachers, the number and variety can be confusing. In short, a
framework is needed to integrate the various approaches. In this
book I attempt to provide that context. To accomplish this task I
have organized teaching approaches with respect to their orientation and the amount of structure associated with each model.
Humanizing the Classroom attempts to fill a gap in the literature on
affective education, since to date there has been no work which
synthesizes the different approaches within a conceptual framework that is also useful to teachers. Within the framework I have
chosen, I have also attempted to present the models in a way that
retains their respective focus: for that purpose I have quoted
liberally from works associated with the models. My hope is that
this book can facilitate an understanding of the approaches and
provide a means for using them effectively in the classroom.

The book should be useful to teachers at a number of levels.
For example, it should be relevant to instructors of university
courses in curriculum and instruction in a variety of areas (for
example, general curriculum, social studies methods, English
education), since the teaching approaches can be used in many
subject areas in the school curriculum. The book should also be
useful to teachers at other levels who seek an introduction to
affective education. Some of the approaches are applicable to the
secondary and post-secondary levels, other approaches are aimed

v

at the elementary classroom, while a few of the models can be used in almost any setting. Although the focus is on education, readers interested in the human potential movement and transpersonal psychology may also find the book of interest, since many of the techniques described can be applied to personal growth and integration outside the classroom.

Affective education is still in its infancy. Other teaching approaches are being developed and the overall direction of humanistic education is still being defined. Despite its infant state, the climate for affective education has changed in the last few years. A few years ago it was unheard of to consider the use of meditation in schools, but today meditation is used in a variety of educational settings. The individuals associated with the approaches discussed in the book have helped bring about this new climate. They have helped create an atmosphere in which students and teachers can explore their feelings and intuitions. We are indebted to their pioneering efforts. I hope that this text, along with the existing works in affective education, can build on their efforts so that educational environments become more fully conducive to human development and personal integration.

I want to thank the following individuals who made this book possible: Hugh Oliver, of the Ontario Institute for Education, who suggested that I write it; Bruce Joyce, David Hunt, and Marsha Weil whose ideas formed the organizing framework for the teaching approaches described in the text; and Gladys Topkis and Herman Makler, of Praeger, who provided both sincere interest and thoughtful observations on the manuscript.

Finally, I dedicate the book to my wife, Jean, whose support during the writing of the book was invaluable and who also shares an interest in many of the approaches described in the pages that follow.

J.P.M.

CONTENTS

CHAPTER 1
WHY AFFECTIVE EDUCATION?

The news media constantly present us with data on student alienation. The high rates of dropouts, suicides, alcohol and drug abuse, and school vandalism are some of the indicators of this social condition.

The frequency of suicide, the most extreme expression of alienation, is difficult to measure because suicide is often reported as an accident. Certain trends are evident, however. In the United States suicide is the second most common cause of death among young people. In Canada suicide among all age groups doubled between 1950 and 1972. Among people aged 15 to 19 and 20 to 24, the rate more than quadrupled and tripled, respectively.

Alcohol and drug use has also increased. In the United States from 1969 to 1972 alcohol use among high-school seniors increased 90 percent. Drug use, which has received more publicity, has also increased during the last decade. In Canada the number of users of narcotics (excluding marijuana) increased 58 percent between 1964 and 1970. The largest increase was in the under-twenty and twenty to twenty-nine age groups.[1]

Some individuals have made a connection between these data and schooling. Herter Berger, Associate Professor of Clinical Medicine at New York Medical College, concluded from a study of 343 drug-addicted youth: "Compulsory education engenders in the individual [drug user] a hatred of society. . . . He attempts to destroy his jail (school). . . . Finally, he attempts a chemical escape (drugs) from his environment."[2]

Of course, the school is not the sole cause of this situation.

1

Exposure to other societal forces through the mass media is also conducive to alienation. Viewing trips to the moon, war in the Middle East, starvation in Africa, can numb or desensitize the individual. Douglas Heath, who has been studying student alienation for the past quarter century, suggests how television can inhibit expression of feelings:

> Television must go way out—to the more intense, perverse, or bizarre—in order to stay "in." Now, each of us knows that when we see violence, for example, we become tense and perhaps even a little angry ourselves. Since most middle-class families do not permit children to hit each other, they have few ways by which to express their aroused tensions. They learn to inhibit their feelings. After thousands of hours of this conditioning does not one become insensitive to the massacres at Pinkville and does not one need the release of marijuana? [3]

The increased divorce rate and the concomitant restructuring of the nuclear family is another factor that influences the alienation trend. Children who must cope with a marital split attempt to insulate themselves emotionally. Certain phrases betray this value of insulation: "Stay cool," "Don't get uptight," "Don't freak." The young, then, repress their feelings in order to maintain a cool facade, or lose themselves in the loud vibrations of rock music.

In his research on the trend of alienation, Heath has discovered, for example, that students show signs of increasing isolation. Over a twenty-year period he collected the following responses from seventeen-year-old males:[4]

	PERCENTAGE AGREEING					
	1948	1952	1956	1960	1964	1968
"When I was a child I didn't care to be a member of a crowd or gang."	33	35	35	38	49	47
"I could be happy living all alone in a cabin in the woods or mountains."	23	28	31	38	33	45
"My worries seem to disappear when I get into a crowd of lively friends."	71	69	73	68	58	55

These data indicate to Dr. Heath a growing estrangement and loneliness among the young, because they increasingly prefer isolation and detachment.

Ivan Illich, Edgar Friedenberg, John Holt, and Jonathan Kozol, as well as many other writers, have documented how certain features of schooling such as compulsory attendance, communication patterns, and role selection make it difficult for students to develop a genuine sense of identity. The trend toward larger schools, particularly at the secondary level, has also contributed to student alienation. Research indicates that students in large schools encounter their friends less often and have less contact with adults than students in smaller schools. They participate in fewer activities and hold fewer positions of responsibility, are more competitive, and develop a narrower conception of their own worth. There is also a correlation between large schools and the frequency of cheating.[5]

Many students respond to impersonal schooling by dropping out. A study conducted in London, Ontario, to investigate an increase in dropouts among secondary students from 5.4 percent to 9.6 percent over a five-year period, classified students on the basis of their interview responses as either "hassled" or "okay." About 48 percent of the students were classified as "hassled" and 52 percent as "okay." In other words, almost half the students were alienated.

The study suggested to the investigator, A. Mikalachki, that teachers should attempt to become more aware of students' feelings and should use classroom strategies that relate to the affective concerns of youth. Mikalachki concludes:

> It appears that cognitive learning does not take into account either the feelings and concerns of the student or the social environment that affects those feelings and concerns. But, as our study demonstrates, they have their inevitable consequences. Cognitive learning cannot take place in a state of affective disorder, and we can no longer assume that the family or some other agency will take responsibility for the student's affective development. It is imperative that school systems devote both their wits and their financial resources to the production of programs of affective learning. In them lies a response not only to youth alienation but also to many other human problems that challenge the educational system in this decade.[6]

Traditionally, the schools have focused on cognitive skills. Education of the emotions, if it is suggested at all, is treated as a side issue with little relevance to the school's core program. Limitation of time and an uneasiness about dealing openly with feelings are typical reasons for not developing programs in affective education. This uneasiness was illustrated during a seminar conducted by Carl Rogers at a large university in the United States shortly after the campus had been disrupted by student demonstrations. After a while, one of the faculty members, a physicist, began to move his chair away from the small group. Dr. Rogers commented that he felt the professor was withdrawing from the group. The professor responded that he was withdrawing because he had come to the conference to learn, and said:

> **"Learning takes place on an intellectual, rational level, not on an emotional plane. Not a wise intellectual statement has been uttered here today. If anyone else would care to engage in an intellectual discussion, I propose they leave this group and join me in the next room for some profitable learning."** [7]

After that statement, another member of the group responded that he now had better insight into some problems at the university, since he felt that refusal to deal with the emotions contributes to student alienation and campus disruptions. The physicist's response was understandable, however, because very few educational institutions have developed a climate in which members can deal with their feelings openly.

The following not atypical incident shows how an elementary-school teacher failed to deal with affect.

TEACHER: Now we will open our books and do the ten problems on page 33.
JOHNNY: I don't feel like it.
TEACHER: Johnny, open your book and get started.
JOHNNY: I hate math!
TEACHER: Get started now, or I am going to give you extra work.
JOHNNY: I'm not going to do it.[8]

In a large number of classrooms Flanders and Amidon found that acceptance of feelings accounted for only .005 percent of the verbal interaction in the classroom.[9] There are many teachers, however, who are interested in increasing their guidance skills and abilities to facilitate the children's emotional growth.[10] It is hoped that this book will assist elementary- and secondary-school teachers who share this interest.

Several teaching strategies are presented here which are intended to humanize the classroom environment. They are offered in a theoretical context so that they might be effective in a variety of teaching circumstances. Although each model has a different focus, their over-all aim is to reduce student alienation and facilitate personal integration.

What is meant by personal integration? First, the personally integrated individual is committed to growth and development. He sees his life as a process of becoming and attempts to choose experiences that are conducive to that development. Thus he is willing to take risks and face conflict, since he knows that without risks his development may be arrested. In short, he has a sense of developmental change.

He also has a sense of identity. He can define the values he believes in and can openly affirm those values that are integral to his identity. Although he is sensitive to the needs of others, the identity he has developed is his own and is not based on what others expect of him. It is based on a conscious process of choice and self-determination.

The integrated person is open and sensitive to the needs of others. He does not cut himself off from people, and he can clearly communicate an empathy for others. He can function effectively in a group situation.

Finally, personal integration represents a unity of consciousness. The individual feels a balance between heart and mind. He experiences a sense of wholeness; he can exercise his intuitive and imaginative faculties as well as his rational capabilities. This balance of consciousness has been aptly called the informed heart.[11]

Affective education attempts to develop one or more of these components of personal integration. The term "humanistic education" is often used interchangeably with "affective education," as are "confluent education" and "psychological education." In this text, the two latter terms do not have this comprehensive meaning but refer to specific teaching approaches.

It would be naïve to suggest that affective education alone can bring about personal integration. The models presented in this text will be most effective in a school where the "hidden curriculum"—that is, the implicit rules and norms—is openly examined and integrated with explicit aims that include personal integration. The community surrounding the school should be supportive of personal integration as an aim. However, even if the community is more concerned with basic skills, it is my belief that the three R's cannot be detached from affective development. A person with a low conception of himself or with negative feelings about school will have a difficult time learning even the most basic skills. In short, the teacher cannot afford to fragment the curriculum into solely cognitive or affective components, or the student will not develop either skill mastery or personal integration.

Notes

1. Marshall Wilensky, "Self-Destructive Behavior," *Orbit* 6, no. 2 (April 1975): 7–9.
2. Quoted in Ralph Mosher and Norman Sprinthall, "Psychological Education in the Secondary Schools," *American Psychologist* 25 (October 1970): 911.
3. Douglas Heath, "Student Alienation and the School," *School Review* 78, no. 4 (August 1970): 524.
4. Douglas Heath, *Humanizing Schools* (New York: Hayden Book Co., 1971), p. 21.
5. Heath, "Student Alienation and the School," p. 526.
6. A. Mikalachki, "Youth Alienation and the School System," *Orbit* 4, no. 5 (1973): 19.
7. Quoted in Harold Lyons, *Learning to Feel—Feeling to Learn* (Columbus, Ohio: Charles Merrill, 1971), p. 22.
8. Don Dinkmeyer, "Top Priority: Understanding Self and Others," *Elementary School Journal* 72, no. 2 (1971): 64.
9. N. A. Flanders and E. J. Amidon, "The Role of the Teacher in the Classroom" (Minneapolis, Minn.: Minneapolis Association for Productive Teaching, 1967).
10. M. Witmee and H. Cottingham, "The Teacher's Role and Guidance Functions as Reported by Elementary Teacher," *Elementary School Guidance and Counseling* 5 (October 1970): 12–22.
11. Bruno Bettelheim, *The Informed Heart* (New York: Avon, 1971).

BIBLIOGRAPHY

Friedenberg, Edgar. *Coming of Age in America.* New York: Random House, 1965. Contains some interesting research on student alienation in the secondary schools.

Holt, John. *How Children Fail.* New York: Dell, 1964. A classic text on student alienation in the elementary school.

Jackson, Philip. *Life in the Classrooms.* New York: Holt, Rinehart & Winston, 1968. A short yet powerful analysis of alienation in the schools.

Jones, Richard M. *Fantasy and Feeling in Education.* New York: Harper & Row, 1968. Jones analyzes theories of instruction which ignore feelings and imagination. In particular, he focuses on Bruner's "Man: A Course of Study."

Lyon, Harold. *Learning to Feel—Feeling to Learn.* Columbus, Ohio: Charles Merrill, 1971. Lyon presents a number of affective teaching techniques, with their rationales. He also discusses a number of pioneer figures in humanistic education.

McPherson, Gertrude. *Small Town Teacher.* Cambridge, Mass.: Harvard University Press, 1972. An excellent analysis of alienation in the schools. Although the subject is a school in a small community, the implications of the analysis go beyond this context.

CHAPTER 2
MODELS OF TEACHING IN AFFECTIVE EDUCATION

The aim of this book is to provide a practical guide for individuals seeking teaching strategies to facilitate the personal integration of their students. Some of the strategies may already be familiar to the teacher, but they are presented here in a theoretical context so that they can be applied in a variety of teaching circumstances. The organization is derived from the work of Bruce Joyce, Marsha Weil, and David Hunt.

Central to the organization is Joyce and Weil's concept of a teaching model: "a pattern or plan which can be used to shape a curriculum or course, to select instructional materials, and to guide a teacher's actions." They add: "As we describe models and discuss their uses, we will find that the task of selecting an appropriate model is complex and that the forms of 'good' teaching are numerous, depending on our purposes."[1] Teaching is seen as a process in which teacher and students together create an environment that reflects certain values and beliefs. Thus each model embodies specific values and beliefs about human nature and provides a frame of reference for developing classroom activities.

In their book, *Models of Teaching*, Joyce and Weil present a number of models covering many areas—social interaction, behavior modification, information processing, and others. In this book the focus is more specifically on affective education. The affective teaching models selected for discussion in this book have a theoretical base, a clear and identifiable rationale for their use. Further, they specify a set of strategies for classroom application. The models, then, stand up to the realities of classroom interaction. Since the focus of this book is practical, I have emphasized the latter criterion in discussing the various models. The reader can consult the original source if he or she desires more information about the model's rationale.

There is no one best way of teaching that is applicable in all situations. The teacher's task is to select the model that will be most effective in a given set of circumstances. Basically, there are two factors involved in selecting a teaching model. First, the model must meet the teacher's goal and concern. For example, if the concern is to facilitate a positive identity, one of the models in the self-concept family (Chapter 4) deserves the teacher's attention. Second, the model must relate to the amount of structure the students can handle. Some students require an environment with a good deal of structure and direction; others are comfortable in situations with more flexibility and ambiguity. Similarly, some teaching models provide a high degree of structure (e.g., values clarification), while others provide an environment that is more fluid and unstructured (self-directed model). The task of the teacher, then, is to match the appropriate teaching model to learner characteristics.

To clarify the purpose and focus of each model, they have been grouped into four families: (1) *developmental* models, (2) *self-concept* models, (3) *sensitivity* and *group-orientation* models, and (4) *consciousness-expansion* models. These categories are not meant to be rigid; some models, such as the role-playing model, could be grouped under two or more of the headings. The categories do serve to indicate the principal focus of the model within the general framework of personal integration.

Chapter 3, then, includes models that outline approaches to affective education within a developmental perspective. The classroom strategies are linked to a particular stage in the learner's life span, so that affective education strategies are developmentally appropriate. For example, Hoffman and Ryan describe a number of teaching strategies within their framework of psychosocial development.

The second family of models, presented in Chapter 4, focus on the self and the development of personal identity. These models

Table 1

AFFECTIVE TEACHING MODELS

	Model	Theorist(s)	Orientation	Aims
1.	Ego development	Erikson	Developmental	Resolution of ego crises
2.	Psychological model	Mosher and Sprinthall	Developmental	Facilitation of ego, cognitive, and moral development
3.	Psychosocial model	Ryan and Hoffman	Developmental	Positive self-concept and independent learning skills
4.	Moral development model	Kohlberg	Developmental	Avoidance of stage retardation
5.	Values clarification	Simon, Raths, Kirschenbaum and Harmin	Self-concept	Incorporation of valuing process
6.	Identity education	Weinstein and Fantini	Self-concept	Positive identity, self-control, and relatedness to others
7.	Classroom meeting model	Glasser	Self-concept	Sense of identity through responsible decision making
8.	Role-playing model	Shaftel and Shaftel	Self-concept	Positive self-concept, group cohesiveness, and problem-solving skills
9.	Self-directed model	Rogers	Self-concept	Fully functioning person
10.	Communication model	Carkhuff	Sensitivity and group	Communications skills
11.	Sensitivity-consideration model	McPhail	Sensitivity and group	Awareness of others' needs and feelings
12.	Transactional analysis	Harris, Berne and Ernst	Sensitivity and group	Open communication and personal growth
13.	Human relations training	National Training Laboratory	Sensitivity and group	Interpersonal skills

Model	Theorist(s)	Aims	Orientation
14. Meditation	Ornstein	Consciousness expansion	Awareness and centeredness
15. Synectics	Gordon	Consciousness expansion	Creative and imaginative capacities
16. Confluent education	Castillo, Brown and Hillman	Consciousness expansion	Integration and holistic perception
17. Psychosynthesis	Assagioli and Crampton	Consciousness expansion	Integration through centeredness

have a strong personalistic emphasis. They help the individual clarify his thoughts and feelings about who he is and how his values reflect his self-perception. For example, teaching strategies in values clarification have a personalistic focus in order to facilitate the student's ability to clarify his thinking about personal values.

The third set of models (Chapter 5) facilitate openness and sensitivity to others. Often group work is conducive to this aspect of personal integration. Human relations training, for example, attempts to facilitate the student's awareness of others and his ability to incorporate this awareness in group functioning.

The final set of strategies, presented in Chapter 6, concerns methods of consciousness expansion. Evidence has recently been found that the human brain consists of two hemispheres.[2] The left hemisphere controls language, rational cognition, and analytical thought. The right side in most cases seems to be responsible for intuition, fantasy, and other nonrational forms of consciousness. Relatively speaking, the latter mode of consciousness has been little developed in Western culture, and the strategies discussed in Chapter 6 attempt to facilitate consciousness expansion in this sphere. The models and their respective orientations and goals are listed in Table 1.

Once the teacher has decided on the major aim of teaching, he or she then should attempt to match the teaching model to what David Hunt and his colleagues call *conceptual level* (CL), the level of structure at which the students operate. In Hunt's model there are four conceptual levels for the individual and four corresponding learning environments. These conceptual levels and learning environments can be summarized as follows:[3]

Table 2

CHARACTERISTICS OF STAGE	OPTIMAL TRAINING ENVIRONMENT
I. Stage I is characterized by fixed patterns of response. The individual tends to see things evaluatively—that is, in terms of rights and wrongs—and he tends to categorize the world in terms of stereotypes. He prefers unilateral social relationships—that is, those that are hierarchical and in which some people are on top and others on the bottom. He tends to reject information that does not fit in with his present belief system, or to distort the information in order to store it in his existing categories.	In order to produce development from this stage, the training environment needs to be fairly well structured, because this kind of person will become even more rigid under an overly open social system. At the same time, however, the environment has to stress delineation of the personality in such a way that the individual begins to see himself as distinct from his beliefs and begins to recognize that different people have different vantages from which they look at the world and that the rights, wrongs, and rules in a situation can be negotiated. The optimal environment for him, then, is supportive, structured, and fairly controlling, but with a stress on self-delineation and negotiation.
II. In Stage II, the individual is breaking away from the rigid rules and beliefs that characterized his Stage I. He is in a state of active resistance to authority and tends to oppose control from all sources, even nonauthoritative ones. He still tends to dichotomize the environment. He has difficulty seeing the points of view of others, and maintaining a balance between task orientation and interpersonal relations.	In this stage, the delineation of self is taking place, and the individual needs to begin to re-establish ties with others, to begin to take on the points of view of others, and to see how they operate in situations. Consequently, the training environment needs to emphasize negotiation in interpersonal relations and divergence in the development of rules and concepts.

CHARACTERISTICS OF
STAGE *(cont.)*

OPTIMAL TRAINING
ENVIRONMENT *(cont.)*

III. At Stage III, the individual is beginning to re-establish easy ties with other people, beginning to take on the point of view of others, and in his newfound relationships with other people has some difficulty maintaining a task orientation because of his concern with the development of interpersonal relations. He is, however, beginning to balance alternatives and to build concepts that bridge differing points of view and ideas that apparently contradict each other.

The training environment at this point should strengthen the re-established interpersonal relations, but emphasis should also be placed on tasks in which the individual has to proceed toward a goal as a member of the group as well as maintain himself with other individuals. If the environment is too protective, the individual could be arrested at this stage and, while he might continue to develop skill in interpersonal relations, would be unlikely to develop further skill in conceptualization or to maintain himself in task-oriented situations.

IV. The Stage IV individual is able to maintain a balanced perspective with respect to task orientation and the maintenance of interpersonal relations. He can build new constructs and beliefs or belief systems as necessary to accommodate to changing situations and new information. In addition, he is able to negotiate with others the rules or conventions that will govern behavior under certain situations and can work with others to set out programs of action and conceptual systems for approaching abstract problems.

While this individual is adaptable, he no doubt operates best in an interdependent, information-oriented, complex environment.

Individuals operating at Stage I require a high degree of structure; at Stages II and III, a moderate amount of structure; and at Stage IV, a low degree of structure. To be maximally effective the teacher should not only attempt to match the model to the learner's CL but also create a situation where the student can gradually learn to handle more complexity and ambiguity. If the student is at Stage I, then, there should eventually be an attempt to facilitate movement into Stage II.

Carl Rogers, in *Freedom to Learn,* describes a situation in which a sixth-grade teacher recognized differing conceptual levels in her class and structured the classroom situation to meet these differing needs. She set up a "contract system" in which the individual student with the teacher contracted a work plan within the prescribed curriculum. After a while the teacher realized that some students needed more structure, so she set up two groups to meet these needs.

> Some children continued to to be frustrated and felt insecure without teacher direction. Discipline also continued to be a problem with some, and I began to realize that although the children involved may need the program more than the others, I was expecting too much from them, too soon—they were not ready to assume self-direction yet. Perhaps a gradual weaning from the spoon-fed procedures was necessary.
>
> I regrouped the class—creating two groups. The largest group is the non-directed. The smallest is teacher-directed, made up of children who wanted to return to the former teacher-directed method, and those who, for varied reasons, were unable to function in the self-directed situation. . . .
>
> Those who continued the "experiment" have forged ahead. I showed them how to program their work, using their texts as a basic guide. They have learned that they can teach themselves (and each other) and that I am available when a step is not clear or advice is needed. . . .
>
> Some of the members of the group working with me are most anxious to become "independent" students. We will evaluate together each week their progress toward that goal. . . .
>
> Some students (there were two or three) who originally wanted to return to the teacher-directed program are now anticipating going back into the self-directed program. (I sense that it has been difficult for them to readjust to the old program as it would be for me to do so.)[4]

This teacher has done what I recommend: she has diagnosed the approximate conceptual level of her students, matched an appropriate teaching model to student needs, and gradually allowed for student transition to a higher stage of development.

Hunt has developed a test to ascertain the learner's CL. However, a sensitive teacher familiar with Hunt's model can probably diagnose CL and identify a corresponding learning environment without administering the test.

The models in this book can be used for a number of purposes. First, they can help the teacher plan his other classroom activities from day to day. Each model has a set of steps that guide lesson planning. The models can be used in the initial stages of work and, when the teacher is familiar with the teaching strategies, he can begin to develop his own approaches and even his own set of models. (The models are presented here in outline form with a few sample strategies. The reader should feel free to go to the original source for more detail and other teaching strategies. A short bibliography is listed at the end of each chapter along with related models, since I have not been able to include all models of teaching in affective education in this book.)

Since each teaching model lends itself to certain instructional materials, the models can also help the teacher select and develop filmstrips, films, and other resource materials.

Finally, the models can help shape a curriculum. Since each model has a rationale and set of objectives, the teacher or curriculum planner can use the models to help clarify his own objectives and instructional means to meet those objectives. In the day of accountability the teacher using the models format would be better able to support and justify his program than a teacher using an ad hoc approach. This is particularly important for affective education programs, which are often exposed to scrutiny and criticism.

ORGANIZATION OF THE BOOK

In each chapter I present a few models that focus on one of the components of personal integration: developmental change, identity realization, consciousness expansion, and sensitivity to others. Each model is presented within the following framework. THEORETICAL ORIENTATION. In this section the goals and assumptions of the model are presented. The rationale behind the model is sometimes explained. CLASSROOM APPLICATION. Here I outline how the model may be used in the classroom, including the specific acts the teacher engages in to implement the teaching approach. (I use the term "teacher" rather loosely in the book. In affective education the teacher is often a facilitator who sets a climate for learning.)

THE TEACHER'S ROLE.   In this category certain principles of action and climate-setting are outlined that are essential to the teacher/facilitator role. In some of the models the teacher is accepting and nondirective; with other approaches, he is more directive and assertive. If the teacher needs access to certain resources and support facilities, this is also mentioned.

APPLICABILITY OF THE MODEL.   Applicability refers to aspects of the approach that facilitate its use in the classroom and other elements that may limit its use. I also venture some personal opinions about the approaches in this section, although in general I have attempted to present the models objectively. These two factors are not complementary, however, as brevity is not always conducive to objectivity.

THE LEARNING ENVIRONMENT.   In this section the short- and long-term effects of the model are discussed. Some aspects of the model are intended to have direct instructional effects (e.g., skills and content), while other aspects of the model's environment are more indirect and nurturant (e.g., values and capacities). The psychological model, for example, instructs the adolescent about the nature of human development. However, in different laboratory settings, such as counseling and theater improvisation, the adolescent's moral and emotional development is nurtured by this model. An understanding of the instructional/nurturant effects can give the teacher more realistic expectations concerning the outcomes of the model. If most of a model's effects are nurturant, it is unrealistic to anticipate immediate outcomes.

Since the concept of structure is central to the organization of the models, it is discussed throughout the book. The amount of structure associated with each model is mentioned in the chapter introductions and summaries and in the presentation of the model itself.

In general this book should be seen as a beginning point for teachers interested in affective education. The teacher can try out the various approaches and select those models that are most effective for him or her. Eventually, the teacher can integrate some of the approaches or even develop his own model of teaching.

Notes

1. Bruce Joyce and Marsha Weil, *Models of Teaching* (Englewood Cliffs, N.J.: Prentice-Hall, 1972), p. 3.
2. See Robert Ornstein, *The Psychology of Consciousness* (New York: Viking Press, 1972).
3. Adapted from ibid., pp. 303–5. Used with permission.
4. Quoted in Carl Rogers, *Freedom to Learn* (Columbus, Ohio: Charles Merrill, 1969), pp. 15–16.

BIBLIOGRAPHY

Hunt, David. *Matching Models in Education.* Toronto: Ontario Institute for Studies in Education, 1971. Hunt describes his conceptual systems model and applies it to schools and teacher training.

Joyce, Bruce, and Weil, Marsha. *Models of Teaching.* Englewood Cliffs, N.J.: Prentice-Hall, 1972. A highly recommended text in curriculum and instruction. Models of teaching are presented in four areas: social interaction, information processing, personal sources, and behavior modification.

CHAPTER 3
DEVELOPMENTAL MODELS

The theme of this chapter is developmental change, since each teaching model outlines a sequence of human development. Generally, the teacher's task is to try to identify where the student is on the developmental continuum and to choose an appropriate set of activities for that point and each subsequent developmental stage. The models in this chapter reflect the assumption that no one teaching model is suitable for all stages of development, but that different approaches should be used to correspond to the learners' developmental levels.

These models can also give the teacher an overview of human development and thus shape programs that are conducive to learning and growth. Kohlberg, for example, suggests that developmental theory can provide a basic rationale and direction for humanistic programs of education.[1]

The adolescent student can study these theories in order to gain a sense of developmental change, to see himself in the process of development. This perspective is often conducive to personal integration.

Erikson's well-known theory details eight succeeding periods of *emotional and ego development.* Although not directly concerned with education, his theory and concepts have implications for teaching and for affective education. The concept of psychosocial moratorium, for example, is relevant to educational environments for adolescents.

Kohlberg's *theory of moral development* has become a widely accepted model of moral education. Derived originally from the work of Piaget, Kohlberg's model defines six stages of development and suggests strategies to facilitate development and moral reasoning.

While the work of Erikson and of Kohlberg spans the life cycle, the other two models in this chapter focus on specific phases. Thus Hoffman and Ryan have developed a *model of psychosocial growth* that is relevant to the elementary school years. They discuss four stages, and suggest that most elementary school students are in two of these stages. The work of Mosher and Sprinthall, which they call *"psychological education,"* because their model integrates several teaching approaches around the concept of personal development, focuses on adolescence.

Because of their developmental focus, each of the four models offers several levels of structure, related to the different stages of development. In general, however, the Erikson and Kohlberg approaches are moderate in structure, the psychosocial model is high-to-moderate, and the psychological-education approach is moderate-to-low.

A MODEL OF EGO DEVELOPMENT

Erik Erikson, a psychoanalyst, has developed a theory of human development which has been useful to professional workers in such behavioral fields as psychotherapy, social work, and education. His work has also inspired constructive social change. During the civil rights movement of the 1960s, many young people testing the constraints of segregation in the South carried his *Childhood and Society* with them through their struggle.

Erikson's conception of the eight stages of man can help the teacher to identify periods of emotional growth in students' lives and respond with activities that are congruent with those periods. Together with the work of Piaget and Kohlberg, Erikson's eight stages can help teachers at all levels to gain a broader, more integrated view of human growth.

The Eight Stages of Man

To use the Erikson model of teaching effectively, it is important for teachers to have an understanding of the various stages of emotional growth.

The first stage (up to age 2) is the period of basic trust versus mistrust. In the child's early relationship with his mother (for example, in the feeding relationship), he learns basic trust by discovering that there is some correspondence between his needs and his immediate environment.

Each Erikson stage describes a "crisis" or emotional tension between two fundamental elements—for example, in the first stage, between trust and mistrust. If the first stage is successfully completed, most of the growth will incorporate a sense of trust. Erikson states, however, that the child should leave each stage with a smaller ratio of the balancing tension—that is, at the end of the first stage, his sense of trust should be tempered with mistrust. In the interest of survival in a rapidly changing society, he should have a sense of being prepared to face danger and discomfort. Developmental crises are not catastrophes but times of heightened vulnerability and potentiality with regard to particular facets of psychosexual development.

The second period (ages 2–4) is the stage of a sense of autonomy versus a sense of shame. During this stage the child gains greater muscular control (e.g., of the sphincter muscles) and as a result develops a sense of autonomy. At this time he attempts to feed himself, to walk, to dress himself, to open and shut things. The parents' task is to grant him gradually increasing independence within sensible limits. If parental control is too restrictive or if the child does not have a sense of muscular control, he may develop lasting feelings of self-doubt and shame.

During the third period (ages 4–7), the stage of initiative versus guilt, the child begins to test his autonomy in a wider, more social context, including a variety of toys, pets, and perhaps a younger sibling. He no longer merely manipulates objects; he begins to undertake projects that require completion. He also begins to realize that he is a person and that he can act purposefully. This realization may lead him to wonder what his work will be and to create fantasies about the active person he wants to become. If he imagines himself as mother or father, or if he goes too far and sees himself impinging on another person's sphere of endeavor, he may develop a sense of guilt. It is the parents' task to broaden his social context in such a way that he is not overwhelmed by these feelings.

Erikson's fourth stage, industry versus inferiority, occurs during middle childhood (ages 7–11). At this point in development, the crisis centers on the child's ability to gain a sense of industry by mastering some of the tools and techniques of his culture. If his experiences are successful, he acquires feelings of competence; if they are not, he develops feelings of inferiority. Since Erikson refers to this period as the "school age," the implication is that the school and teacher have a major role in helping the child develop a sense of industry. They may facilitate the process by creating situations that allow the child to master a variety of tasks.

It is during adolescence that Erikson's well-known fifth stage of identity versus identity diffusion occurs. During this period, identity develops as childhood self-concepts are modified in the light of the anticipated future. If the adolescent relates successfully to his environment, he is at peace with himself, knows where he is going, and is confident of recognition from his immediate community. If he does not, he succumbs to identity confusion and feels like Biff in Arthur Miller's *Death of a Salesman:* "I just can't take hold . . . I can't take hold of some kind of life." As a result he may respond to the conflicts and demands of adolescence by becoming a delinquent or engaging in some other deviant form of behavior.

Beyond adolescence Erikson discusses the stages of intimacy versus isolation, generativity versus self-absorption, and integrity versus despair. During the intimacy-versus-isolation period the young adult must be secure in his own identity so that he can fuse it with someone else's in a mutual relationship without fear of identity loss. It is the development of intimacy and the ability to love that makes a healthy marriage possible. In the adult years, during the crisis of generativity versus self-absorption, the individual sees his life in relation to future generations. If the stage is successfully completed, he has a sense that his work (e.g., child care, teaching, the building of ideas and tools) has meaning in terms of the development of future generations. If not, his tasks lose generational significance and are relevant only to the self. The final crisis, in old age, is integrity versus despair, in which the individual must come to terms with his own death in the light of his past life cycle. In sum, a sense of integrity comes from the realization that one has led a fulfilled life and has successfully resolved past crises. A realization of lack of fulfillment leads to despair or disgust.

Classroom Application

The first step in using the Erikson model is for the teacher to identify approximately the child's stage of emotional growth. This is done mainly through observation. The teacher then chooses activities that are appropriate to that period of development. For example, Erikson points out the importance of play during the early-childhood periods of autonomy and initiative. Play for him is the "infantile ability to create model situations and to master reality by experiment and planning."[2] Erikson quotes from *Tom Sawyer* to make his point. Here, Tom is whitewashing a fence while Ben Rogers "plays" at being captain.

> He took up his brush and went tranquilly to work. Ben Rogers hove in sight presently—the very boy, of all boys, whose ridicule he had been dreading. Ben's gait was the hop-skip-and-jump— proof enough that his heart was light and his anticipations high. He was eating an apple, and giving a long, melodious whoop, at intervals, followed by a deep-toned ding-dong-dong, ding-dong-dong, for he was personating a steamboat. As he drew near, he slackened speed, took the middle of the street, leaned far over to starboard and rounded to ponderously and with laborious pomp and circumstance—for he was personating the Big Missouri, and considered himself to be drawing nine feet of water. He was boat and captain and engine bells combined, so he had to imagine himself standing on his own hurricane-deck giving the orders and executing them.[3]

Erikson then comments on the meaning of Ben's play.

> One "meaning" of Ben's play could be that it affords his ego a temporary victory over his gangling body and self by making a well-functioning whole out of brain (captain), the nerves and muscles of will (signal system and engine), and the whole bulk of the body (boat). It permits him to be an entity within which he is his own boss, because he obeys himself.[4]

Play, then, allows the child to gain ego strength during early childhood, and the teacher of children at this level should create environments so that play can occur.

For youngsters in middle childhood, it is important to provide a wide variety of concrete materials so that they can gain a sense of industry and competence. Erikson himself taught in Vienna as a young man, and his work there gives some hint of the kind of learning environment that facilitates emotional growth. Robert Coles has described the school where Erikson taught:

> He and Peter Blos were given full freedom to organize a curriculum and teach it, a necessary gift from people who appreciated more than many the importance of such freedom to both children and teachers. The result was what I suppose could be called a progressive school, similar in certain respects to some American experimental schools. The children were not graded. They were taught as individuals. They themselves were encouraged to teach, to share in planning the day's activities and choosing the subject matter. If there was conventional matter to be learned conventionally—languages, facts and axioms—there was also a good deal of the adventuresome to be met, and taken in not as something required, but something chosen and enjoyable.
>
> The children worked with both their minds and their hands. Herr Erik, as he was called, taught them how to draw and paint, how to put together a collection of poems and songs, or a yearbook. He also taught them history, and not only German history. They read about Eskimos and American Indians, and they poured their impressions into compositions and pictures. They also made a variety of tools, toys and exhibits, so as to give each culture they studied some flesh. . . .
>
> Yet the teachers did not overlook the need children have for a sense of order, for controls that make things work but don't senselessly intimidate.[5]

This description, although brief, is reminiscent of descriptions of the British infant school by Lillian Weber[6] and Joseph Featherstone,[7] in that all three emphasize an informal atmosphere where the children are actively involved with a wide variety of materials.

During adolescence two concepts associated with the identity-versus-diffusion crisis have meaning in an educational context. The first is the concept of ideology; the second, the concept of what Erikson calls the psychosocial moratorium.

Erikson defines ideology as a world view, a set of significant values, or simply a way of life that exists within a particular culture. If the various ideologies of a culture are meaningful to the adolescent, he can develop ideological commitment. If they are not, he may suffer from a confusion of values. Erikson cites

George Bernard Shaw's adolescent commitment to Fabian social-
ism to show how ideological commitment can help a young person to channel his energies and prepare for the tasks of
adulthood.

Teachers can facilitate identity formation by discussing alternative ideologies with their students, presenting various world
views or significant sets of values for them to explore in relation
to their own experience. The teacher, of course, should not influence his students to adopt a particular set of values but should
respect their autonomy in choosing and defending their own
ideology. The teacher's role is to provide information and to
probe and provoke the students' ability to define and defend
their ideological commitments.

Erikson uses the term "psychosocial moratorium" to mean a
relaxation of institutional pressures that allows the adolescent to
find himself through role experimentation. As an example, Erikson refers to his own "moratorium" when he became an artist
and traveled through Europe. In terms of education, a moratorium suggests flexibility that enables the student to commit himself
temporarily to alternative roles. The SEED program in Toronto
and the Philadelphia Parkway program, for example, permit secondary-school students to explore the city and its various agencies. The Parkway program encourages students to study and
work in such cooperating institutions as the city police depart-
ment, the district attorney's office, the Philadelphia chapter of
the American Civil Liberties Union, the municipal zoo, the In-
surance Company of North America, the Franklin Institute, and
Smith, Kline and French, a leading drug manufacturer. These
temporary involvements allow the students to clarify their thinking about vocational commitments—a primary aspect of identity
formation.

Some schools have developed individual courses that offer opportunities for direct contact with areas of community concern
and, as a result, contribute to the growth of identity. The "Community and I" course at Thornlea School in Toronto is an example. After reviewing community problems with their teachers, the
students form common-interest groups to study and perhaps take
action on particular problems of their choice. Since four periods
a day are devoted to this work, students have ample opportunity
for direct exposure to community affairs and for role experimentation.

The Teacher's Role

On occasion, Erikson has spoken directly of the teacher's responsibility in relation to the development of students. In particular he has referred to the concept of negative identity and its educational implications. During adolescence the young person may adopt an identity that is the reverse of his parents' expectations. Instead of being the good boy his parents want him to be, he may become a delinquent or a dropout. If the teacher accepts this negative identity as a matter of convenience, Erikson warns, "the young person may well devote his energy to becoming exactly what the careless and fearful community expects him to be—and make a total job of it."[8] On the strength of his clinical background, Erikson contends that if the negative identity of the adolescent is understood and handled properly, this identity need not be the final one.

Erikson takes a serious view of the responsibility of teaching—so serious, in fact, that he resigned from the University of California rather than sign an oath of loyalty during the McCarthy era of the early 1950s. His statement of resignation shows his concern for the teacher's ultimate responsibilities to his students:

> For many students, their years of study represent their only contact with thought and theory, their only contact with men who teach them how to see two sides of a question and yet to be decisive in their conclusions, how to understand and yet to act with conviction. Young people are rightfully suspicious and embarrassingly discerning. I do not believe they can remain unimpressed by the fact that the men who are to teach them to think and to act judiciously and spontaneously must undergo a political test; must sign a statement which implicitly questions the validity of their own oath of office; must abrogate "commitments" so undefined that they must forever suspect themselves and one another; and must confess to an "objective truth" which they know only too well is elusive. Older people like ourselves can laugh this off; in younger people, however—and especially in those most important students who are motivated to go into teaching—a dangerous rift may well occur between the "official truth" and those deep and often radical doubts which are the necessary condition for the development of thought.[9]

Erikson states that teachers should try to live and act on the truths they deal with in the classroom. If they do not, the educational process becomes a sham. Commitment, of course, can be a dangerous tool in the hands of those who see only one side of an issue, but Erikson is obviously not referring to that situation. His concern is with the appropriate stance in the midst of open-minded inquiry. In general, this concern should lead the teacher to examine his own life in relation to the processes and values he deals with in the classroom.

Applicability of the Model

The Erikson model has the potential for wide application because of its moderate structure and sound theoretical perspective. However, although many teachers find the model theoretically intriguing, they do not always know how to apply this theory to the classroom. In my view the greatest contribution of Erikson's work is its integration with the developmental theories of Piaget and Kohlberg. These theorists present a broad yet integrated view of the developing child from their respective spheres of thought-cognitive development (Piaget), emotional growth (Erikson), and moral development (Kohlberg). An examination of these theories also reveals conditions for educational settings that are conducive to personal integration.[10]

The Learning Environment

As a learning environment, Erikson's model is nurturant: The teacher creates conditions under which the student can gain the sense of industry and identity he needs in order to resolve developmental crises successfully.

PSYCHOLOGICAL EDUCATION FOR ADOLESCENCE

Ralph Mosher and Norman Sprinthall, psychologists, have developed a model of teaching adolescents called "psychological education." Their approach is rooted in the Piaget, Erikson, and Kohlberg theories of human development, which Mosher and Sprinthall feel can best meet the needs of the growing adolescent. For example, one of the adolescent's needs is to facilitate his or her ability to think in abstract terms. Piaget suggests that during adolescence the individual can reach the stage of formal opera-

Figure 1

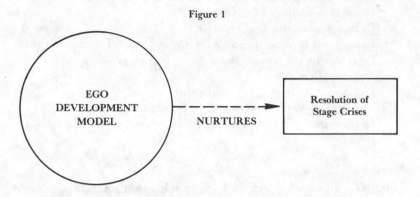

tions in which he can consider many possible solutions to a given problem. Similarly, it is during adolescence, Kohlberg states, that the individual can move to conventional moral reasoning, basing moral judgments on the approval of others or the laws of the society. Finally, Erikson claims that adolescents need to develop a sense of identity, and the Mosher and Sprinthall model attempts explicitly to facilitate identity formation in the secondary-school student. In general, then, the psychological-education model tries to encourage students' growth toward formal operations, conventional moral reasoning, and identity formation. Its aims include

> the development of a more complex and more integrated understanding of oneself; the formation of personal identity; greater personal autonomy; a greater ability to relate to and communicate with other people (e.g., peers and the opposite sex); the growth of more complex ethical reasoning; and the development of more complex skills and competencies—in part by trying prevocational and "adult" roles.[11]

More specifically, the objectives of the model are to enable or assist the individual

> To listen to people—to their ideas and to their feelings.
> To attend to and identify feelings and subjective reactions in general.
> To perceive people accurately and to judge people correctly and efficiently.

To understand himself—who he is at a given time.

To express feelings of his own.

To be spontaneous and creative.

To respond to other people's feelings.

To relate to others—to have more complex, more profound interpersonal relations.

To act in behalf of a personal value.

To perceive—articulate—who he wants to become. . . .

To formulate a set of personal meanings—a personal philosophy.[12]

Classroom Application

The Mosher and Sprinthall approach is embodied in a course in individual and human development for students in grades 11 and 12. The core of the course is essentially cognitive, focusing on the stages of development. Three stages are emphasized: early childhood (the first five years of life), adolescence, and adulthood. The theme of personal history—Who was I as a child? Who am I now? Who am I becoming?—is the focus within this developmental perspective. Besides the personal focus, the students also investigate the work of Piaget, Erikson, and Kohlberg, and other developmental theorists. They read novels and autobiographies dealing with adolescence and see films dealing with it (e.g., "The Loneliness of the Long Distance Runner," "Phoebe," "The Way It Is," and "The Graduate"). Finally, the students read case studies of adolescents such as Inburn, a student described in Keniston's *The Uncommitted*.

Besides the "core" element of the course there are a variety of laboratory activities for students to choose from. The activities include

Film making—biographical and autobiographical films dealing with adolescents.

Teaching—settlement houses, younger children in elementary school.

Volunteer work—mental hospital, hospital, community-action programs.

Student-initiated action projects—for example, Freeport, a residential center for Newton, Mass., adolescents who have left home.

Communication and the art of the motion picture.

Theater improvisation and communication in drama and dance.

Group process—self-analytic groups; seminars involving adolescents, parents, and teachers; sensitivity or T-groups.
Counseling—theories of counseling; study of counseling tapes;
simulated counseling; actual counseling experience.[13]

The course is taught on a team basis so that there are several
resource people for each activity. The student spends about two-
thirds to three-quarters of the total course time in the laboratory
situation, which allows him to experiment with a new role in a
different setting. Erikson argues that free role experimentation is
essential to identity formation; the laboratory activity provides a
setting for this experimentation.

The following experiences are typical of the laboratory activities.

THEATRE IMPROVISATION AND COMMUNICATION. The objectives
of this laboratory experience are "(1) to help students achieve
more self-knowledge through a study of expressive behavior; (2)
to free people to enjoy capacities they might not have known
they had; and (3) to help people learn to relate more effectively
to other people."[14]

Exercises to achieve these objectives involve the skills of speaking and listening. There is also a focus on nonverbal, physical
ways of communicating. In this laboratory, one student learned
through videotapes of movement exercises the relationship between her physical movements and her communication style.
Her reactions to the videotape make this relationship explicit.

"Wow! In the first tape I was so ostentatious and my movements
were wild. I looked like a chipmunk. All over the place. In front
of the camera all the time. Oh, embarrassing. But in the second
tape, I was freer and more real. I can't believe I was so pushy in
the first tape. I liked myself more in the second tape and, you
know, it's because I was more relaxed and could be more of an
individual. First tape—show off! Lousy! Second tape—watching
and listening!"[15]

As a result of concentrating on physical movements and changing her behavior, she learned to watch and listen rather than to
assert and dominate.

Other phases of improvisational drama activity include concentration exercises, exercises that facilitate congruence between emotions and physical movements, and, finally, physical exercises that allow the individual to understand and explore human relations.

LAB IN TEACHING.   In the laboratory activity the student has an opportunity to teach or tutor children in preschool or early grade school. Other students act as teacher aides and assist with small reading groups. Some students help with special skills such as swimming, while others work with exceptional students such as blind or emotionally disturbed children.

After their teaching experiences the students come together with their supervisor to discuss some of the following questions: "(a) What did I teach? (b) What did the child learn? (c) How did I feel? (d) What will I do next? (e) How did the child act?" [16] These discussions allow the student to look at the teaching role, what learning is, and, more importantly, himself or herself as a person.

COUNSELING.   There are three phases to this activity. During the first phase students make tapes in which they counsel other students, parents, and others. Students can learn during this phase to share experiences on a deeper interpersonal level and also to recognize the difficulties in communication. According to Mosher and Sprinthall, "Students also are able to transcend their usual style of communication; that is, to vacate rebellious poses, cliché responses, and to substitute more personal and authentic responses." [17]

Phase two involves testing perceptions. Here the students attempt to compare their perceptions of what other people are saying and feeling with the perceptions of "experts," including people from the educational field, such as counseling psychologists; the work of other experts may be studied through the use of films and tapes. During this phase students can discover that there are no "right" answers and that their perceptions are often supported by the experts.

During phase three the students usually undertake some project that requires a realistic look at expectations and goals and the development of group commitment to the achievement of the project goals. Such a project might involve establishing a residence for students who can no longer live at home, counseling junior-high-school children, or participating in a practicum in counseling for interested adults in the community.

It is evident from a description of a course in psychological education that there are many roles for the teacher. In fact, this teaching model requires a team approach, involving several individuals. The teacher must be flexible and willing to work in a team relationship. It is also important that the teacher have a working knowledge of human development so that he or she can relate laboratory experiences to human development. Certain human skills are also essential. The ability to communicate empathy, genuineness, and respect are particularly important in the counseling laboratory. Each of the laboratory activities, however, requires a different approach. The counseling laboratory is relatively unstructured and requires effective communication skills. Other activities such as teaching are more structured. In general, the Mosher-Sprinthall approach is an attempt to synthesize several models around the common theme of personal development. The activities range in structure from moderate to low.

Applicability of the Model

Since the laboratory activities require a variety of different skills, the number of laboratories is necessarily limited by the size of the staff and the available resources. The staff should be willing to cooperate and work as a team and also to cooperate with and be involved in the community. The staff should establish working relationships with elementary schools and social agencies so that students can have access to these institutions.

Despite the staffing limitations, I feel that this model has great potential for facilitating personal growth. Mosher and Sprinthall

Figure 2

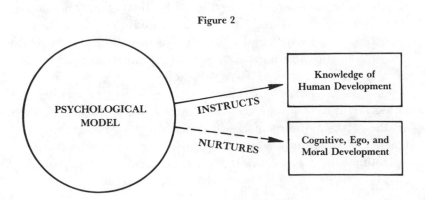

have conducted research on their approach and found that some of the laboratory experiences significantly affect students' ego development, moral development, and communication skills.[18]

The Learning Environment

The psychological model instructs the student about theories in human development. The laboratory phase of the model, however, is nurturant. The laboratories provide a context for facilitating the student's cognitive, ego, and moral development.

A PSYCHOSOCIAL MODEL

This model, which focuses on social and environmental studies, is designed for the elementary-school child. In brief, Alan Hoffman and Thomas Ryan suggest that there are four stages of child development to adolescence. The teacher's task is to be aware of these stages and to match appropriate learning activities to each stage. Hoffman and Ryan have developed a variety of activities for each period of development.

In the *initial exploratory* stage, the infant and preschool child explores the environment. A random thrashing around characterizes this stage. "They keep stretching and moving their arms and legs, trying to figure out, we think, the limits of their world and how they can control these things that they seem to be waving in front of their faces."[19]

Soon the child's environment is structured by parents and siblings. The *structured dependent* stage begins very early and in fact overlaps the initial exploratory stage of development. It lasts until the child is about ten years old. In this stage the child is dependent on adults and siblings to stimulate and structure his activities. Toward the end of this stage the child can begin to choose from the alternatives presented, although the choices are usually determined by parents or teachers.

At around age ten the child becomes more independent of adults. He initiates more activities and has more choices. However, the total environment is still determined by the parents and teacher. This is the *structured independent* stage of development.

Hoffman and Ryan assert that most elementary-school children operate at either the structured dependent or the structured independent level of psychosocial development. A few children, however, reach the fourth level on the continuum: the *independent exploratory* stage. Here the individual can operate independently with regard to his own learning. He no longer requires that the choices be structured but can develop his own set of alternatives.

Each stage is characterized by what Hoffman and Ryan call cross-currents, or themes important to that stage. *Awareness* is the cross-current during the initial exploratory period. Awareness refers to the child's growing perception of himself as a person. During the structured dependent stage the focus is on *consequence,* as the child can begin to see the consequences of certain acts. The third stage focuses on *cause and effect* as the child begins to see broader relationships and patterns of behavior. Finally, *choice* is the dominant cross-current of the independent exploratory stage, as the child can consciously decide what cause-and-effect relationships he wants to establish. The stages and cross-currents are outlined in Table 3.[20]

Classroom Application

As mentioned earlier, Hoffman and Ryan describe a number of activities for each stage. Since most children are at the structured dependent or structured independent stage, the activities discussed here relate to those periods of development.

THE STRUCTURED DEPENDENT STAGE. Some of the experiences at this stage are designed to increase the sense of self. The child is also becoming aware of his "power in relation to others and aware of the power of others in relation to him."[21] One unit develops these themes around the topic of gangs. For example, students are asked to listen to the "Jets' Song" from *West Side Story,* then look at the words of the song on the board. The teacher is told:

> After this, ask the class to underline the reasons why boys joined this gang. (Example: "protected," "never alone," "brothers.")
> a. Are these things necessary?
> b. Are these things provided in any way or by any group other than a gang?
> c. Does a gang assure these things to its members? What is the responsibility of the individual?[22]

Table 3

A MODEL OF THE PSYCHOSOCIAL APPROACH

Stages of Development	Age	Intellectual Abilities	Instructional Strategies
Initial Exploratory	Birth to adult intervention	Awareness	Providing concrete stimuli
Structured Dependent	Adult intervention to approximately age ten	Consequence	Manipulating concrete objects and symbols
Structured Independent	Approximately age ten to development of internalized self	Cause and effect	Labeling and classifying concrete objects and symbols. Making qualitative judgments about both.
Independent Exploratory	Point where child-adolescent can inquire and value independently and abstractly	Choice	Labeling and classifying abstractions. Valuing and inquiring.

Another suggested activity is to show the class a picture of a boy about their age, then tell them that the picture is of a boy in their community who is a member of a gang. The teacher then asks the children why the boy has joined the gang. Finally, the teacher uses role playing to tie together the two previous activities.

Using a set of pictures, have the class act out the situations illustrated. Have pictures not only of the situation, but of people outside the situation. For instance, show a bunch of youths hanging out on a corner. They are members of a gang. In the center, have one boy approaching; identify him as not belonging to this, gang, but to another one. What will happen? Also, have a picture of a neighbor who sees what goes on. Have someone role-play the neighbor and describe her feelings. In this way children will be bringing their own experience and feelings into play. You will be able to distinguish their feelings by the direction they give to the situation. . . .

After each activity discuss the way the players acted—if they were believable, etc. If class desires, have different students act out the same picture, giving it a new interpretation. After each, comment on the motives of the characters and what caused them to act as they did.[23]

STRUCTURED INDEPENDENT STAGE   In relation to this period of development, the concept of exchange facilitates the understanding of cause and effect. A lesson on buying and selling is an example of the activities Hoffman and Ryan suggest.

1. Children are divided into two groups, shoppers and store owners; about 11 shoppers for two stores; each store has two owners.

2. Each shopper receives an equal amount of play money, and all shoppers receive an identical shopping list of items to be obtained at the stores.

3. The stores are provided with play money and goods for the shoppers (pictures from magazines) to buy, but the quantities and prices vary among the stores.

4. The shoppers try to buy all the things on their shopping lists. The shopper who completes his list in the given time is the winner. If there is a tie, the shopper with the most money left over is the winner.

5. The store owners try to sell all their goods at the prices the teacher has set. The store with the most profit is the winner.[24]

Some of the objectives of the lesson are as follows:

1. Children should be able to list the reasons people prefer to shop at one store rather than another.
2. Children should be able to discuss the meaning of "profit" and "competition."
3. Children should be able to discuss why store owners earn an income from their sales and what they must pay for with the income they earn.

After the game there can be discussion relating the role playing to the children's "real-life" shopping experiences. They can also discuss the meaning of "competition," "profit," and "expenses" in relation to the role playing experience.

The Teacher's Role

The teacher using this model should be familiar with the stages of development identified by Hoffman and Ryan so that he can choose the appropriate activities from those outlined by the authors. He can also develop his own set of activities once he is familiar with the model. Hoffman and Ryan also suggest ways in which the teacher can evaluate his effectiveness. The teacher should use evaluation as a means of both diagnosing where the student is and assessing the effectiveness of the curriculum in meeting the student's psychosocial needs.

Most of the activities are either highly structured or moderately structured, depending on the level of student development, so that the activities are appropriate for low- to moderate-CL students.

Applicability of the Model

This approach would appear to have wide applicability because of the structured nature of the activities. However, the model is limited by the conceptual and developmental framework, for the stages are rather vague and poorly defined. Although the stages of development are explained in the first few chapters, the explanations don't always match the activities presented later in the book. For example, the unit on gangs is presented for the *structured dependent* child, but the *structured independent* stage is presented earlier as characterized by high peer involvement. There is no explanation of how the unit on gangs relates specifically to the stage theory. But despite its conceptual inadequacies, the general approach deserves consideration. The teacher will find a number of activities that are practical and usable even if he finds the concepts vague and confusing.

Figure 3

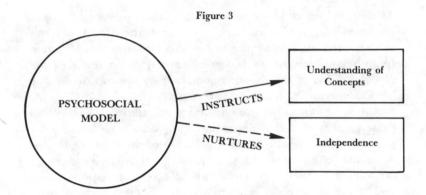

The Learning Environment

The psychosocial model is both instructional and nurturant. It instructs the student in certain developmentally related concepts, such as cause and effect. It also attempts to nurture the student through the stages so that he can pursue learning independently.

A MODEL OF MORAL DEVELOPMENT

Lawrence Kohlberg's theory of moral development describes how people reason about moral issues at different life stages. Kohlberg, a Harvard psychologist, suggests several reasons why a developmental approach to moral education is theoretically sound.[25] First of all, he asserts that the stages of moral reasoning are universal. In research conducted in different cultures, Kohlberg found that individuals pass through the same sequence of development even though the rate of change varies from culture to culture. Since the basic developmental continuum is universal, Kohlberg states that stimulation of the student's moral development is not indoctrinative but simply facilitates what is natural. Kohlberg cites research to support the claim that as individuals move toward higher stages of development they also *act* more honestly and live up to their values. To stimulate moral judgment, then, is also to develop individuals who are more authentic and who act in greater congruence with their beliefs. The stages are outlined below.

I. PRECONVENTIONAL LEVEL

At this level the child is responsive to cultural rules and labels of good and bad, right or wrong, but interprets these labels in terms of either the physical or the hedonistic consequences of action (punishment, reward, exchange of favors) or in terms of the physical power of those who enunciate the rules and labels. The level comprises the following two stages:

STAGE I: *punishment and obedience orientation.* The physical consequences of action determine its goodness or badness regardless of the human meaning or value of these consequences. Avoidance of punishment and unquestioning deference to power are valued in their own right, not in terms of respect for an underlying moral order supported by punishment and authority (the latter being stage 4).

STAGE 2:   *instrumental relativist orientation.* Right action consists of that which instrumentally satisfies one's own needs and occasionally the needs of others. Human relations are viewed in terms similar to those of the marketplace. Elements of fairness, reciprocity, and equal sharing are present, but they are always interpreted in a physical, pragmatic way. Reciprocity is a matter of "you scratch my back and I'll scratch yours," not of loyalty, gratitude, or justice.

II. CONVENTIONAL LEVEL

At this level, maintaining the expectations of the individual's family, group, or nation is perceived as valuable in its own right, regardless of immediate and obvious consequences. The attitude is one not only of *conformity* to personal expectations and social order, but of loyalty to it, of actively *maintaining,* supporting, and justifying the order, and of identifying with the persons or group involved in it. This level comprises the following two stages:

STAGE 3:   *interpersonal concordance or "good boy—nice girl"*

orientation. Good behavior is that which pleases or helps others and is approved by them. There is much conformity to stereotypical images of what is majority or "natural" behavior. Behavior is frequently judged by intention: "he means well" becomes important for the first time. One earns approval by being "nice."
STAGE 4: *"law and order" orientation.* There is orientation toward authority, fixed rules, and the maintenance of the social order. Right behavior consists of doing one's duty, showing respect for authority, and maintaining the given social order for its own sake.

III. POST-CONVENTIONAL, AUTONOMOUS, OR PRINCIPLED LEVEL

At this level there is a clear effort to define moral values and principles that have validity and application apart from the authority of the groups or persons holding these principles and apart from the individual's own identification with these groups. This level again has two stages:
STAGE 5: *social-contract legalistic orientation.* Generally, this stage has utilitarian overtones. Right action tends to be defined in terms of general individual rights and in terms of standards that have been critically examined and agreed upon by the whole society. There is a clear awareness of the relativism of personal values and opinions and a corresponding emphasis on procedural rules for reaching consensus. Aside from what is constitutionally and democratically agreed upon, the right is a matter of personal "values" and "opinion." The result is an emphasis upon the "legal point of view," but with an emphasis upon the possibility of changing law in terms of rational considerations of social utility (rather than freezing it in terms of stage 4 "law and order"). Outside the legal realm, free agreement and contract is the binding element of obligation. This is the "official" morality of the United Stages government and constitution.
STAGE 6: *universal ethical-principle orientation.* Right is defined by the decision of conscience in accord with self-chosen *ethical principles* appealing to logical comprehensiveness, universality, and consistency. These principles are abstract and ethical (the Golden Rule, the categorical imperative); they are not concrete moral rules like the Ten Commandments. At heart, these are universal principles of justice, of the reciprocity and equality of human rights and respect for the dignity of human beings as individual persons.[26]

Central to each stage of development is the concept of what is just or fair for the individual. Each stage's concept of justice or fairness is legitimate for that point in development. The aim of moral education, in Kohlberg's view, is not to accelerate development through the various stages but to avoid stage retardation and to facilitate integration with parallel stages of cognitive and ego development. Research suggests that if children stay at one level for too long, they may get "locked" into that level. For example, an eighteen-year-old at stage 2 is relatively immovable compared to a twelve-year-old at the same stage of development, for he has developed screens and defenses against other perceptions and moral judgments. If the child is not presented with alternative perceptions and judgments, he may become fixated at one stage of development.[27]

Classroom Application

One method of facilitating moral development is to engage the child in moral dilemmas in which there is no "right" answer. In discussing these dilemmas the child can be exposed to different levels of reasoning. The Heinz dilemma, for example, is often used by Kohlberg:

> The drug didn't work, and there was no other treatment known to medicine which could save Heinz's wife, so the doctor knew that she had only about six months to live. She was in terrible pain, but she was so weak that a good dose of pain-killer like ether or morphine would make her die sooner. She was delirious and almost crazy with pain, and in her calm periods, she would ask the doctor to give her enough ether to kill her. She said she couldn't stand the pain and that she was going to die in a few months anyway.
>
> Should the doctor do what she asks and give her the drug that will make her die? Why?[28]

Thoughts about the value of life raised by this dilemma indicate how individuals articulate different levels of moral reasoning. For example, at age ten, Tommy's response to the question is typical of stage 1 thinking. "Is it better to save the life of one important person or a lot of unimportant people? " Tommy answers:

> All the people that aren't important, because one man has just
> one house, maybe a lot of furniture, but a whole bunch of people
> have an awful lot of furniture and some of these poor people
> might have a lot of money and it doesn't look it.[29]

At stage 1 the value of material objects is often confused with the
value of life. As Tommy moves to stage 2 he can distinguish
between the values of material objects and human needs but he
tends to confuse the value of life with individual desires. At age
thirteen Tommy says:

> But the husband wouldn't want his wife to die, it's not like an
> animal. If a pet dies you can get along without it—it isn't some-
> thing you really need. Well, you can get a new wife, but it's not
> really the same.[30]

Here value of life is related to how easily the wife can be re-
placed. Human value is intertwined with convenience to the individual.

At age sixteen Tommy answers the same question:

> It might be best for her, but her husband—it's a human life—not
> like an animal; it just doesn't have the same relationship that a
> human being does to a family; you can become attached to a
> dog, but nothing like a human you know.[31]

Tommy now associates human life with such qualities as love
and empathic relationships; this is typical of stage 3 thinking.

Stage 4 thinking is represented by sixteen-year-old Richard's
thoughts on the value of human life.

> It's not a right or privilege of man to decide who shall live and
> who should die. God put life into everybody on earth and you're
> taking away something from that person that came directly from
> God . . . it's almost destroying a part of God when you kill a
> person.[32]

This is stage 4 thinking because Richard sees the value of human
life in relation to a categorical moral or religious order. Here
moral reasoning is defined by an order maintained by fixed rules
and authority.

At age twenty, Richard's response is representative of stage 5.

It's her own choice. I think there are certain rights and privileges that go along with being a human being. I am a human being and have certain desires for life and I think everybody else does too. You have a world of which you are the center, and everybody else does too and in that sense we're all equal.[33]

Richard now defines the value of life in terms of equal and universal human rights set in a relativistic framework. Later research has indicated that most individuals who attain stage 5 reasoning do so in their mid- to late twenties.

This final response by Richard at age thirty is typical of stage 6 reasoning.

A human life takes precedence over any other moral or legal value, whoever it is. A human life has inherent value whether or not it is valued by a particular individual. The worth of the individual human being is central where the principles of justice and love are normative for all human relationships.[34]

This stage of thinking sees life as an autonomous, universal value that is not dependent on convention or external authority. Most individuals who reach stage 6 thinking do so when they are about thirty years old. Research suggests that only 5 percent of the population reaches stage 6 thinking. On the basis of these data, Kohlberg asserts that moral education should be designed to facilitate post-conventional moral reasoning in adults.

Kohlberg has speculated about a stage 7 orientation in which the individual experiences a fundamental sense of unity with the universe.[35] This sense of unity is an aim of other models discussed later in this book—that is, meditation and psychosynthesis.

As the child participates in discussions of moral dilemmas, he is exposed to different developmental levels. In trying to resolve each conflict or dilemma, he will tend to use the reasoning from the stage above his present level of development. The teacher, then, should present genuine moral conflicts and allow the children to explore them. The teacher should also point out contradictions in the students' thinking, as this also facilitates development.

The teacher should have some feel for the student's current level of development and then create small student groupings so that the student's interaction in the group will expose him to different levels of reasoning and thus facilitate his development. Several research studies have supported the effectiveness of discussing moral dilemmas for moral development.

The teaching process for moral dilemmas involves:

1. Identifying the child's approximate stage of development.
2. Presenting a moral dilemma.
3. Allowing the child to work through the dilemma in a context in which different levels of moral reasoning are evident and the child is presented with reasoning one level above his own.
4. Assisting the child in working through contradictions in his reasoning.

Although developing principles of justice is important to the process of moral development, Kohlberg also acknowledges the importance of empathy and role taking. That is, he does not dismiss the importance of the affective in moral development.

> In contrast, the cognitive-developmental view holds that "cognition" and "affect" are different aspects of, or perspectives on, the same mental events, that all mental events have both cognitive and affective aspects, and that the development of mental dispositions reflects structural changes recognizable in both cognitive and affective perspectives.[36]

Opportunities for role taking also act as a stimulus to moral development. "Research results suggest that all these opportunities for role taking are important and that all operate in a similar direction by stimulating moral development rather than by producing a particular value system."[37]

In order to work through moral dilemmas, the child must be able gradually to see the other person's point of view. If he cannot take the other person's point of view, he cannot develop a conception of what is just or fair for individuals in a moral-conflict situation. At the early stages of moral development, then, there should be opportunities for role playing.

Kohlberg also feels that the school as an environment can facilitate moral development. He and his associates are exploring the concept of the school as a just moral community. Here the administration, staff, and students consciously try to develop a school community around the principle of justice or "fairness." The school's hidden curriculum, or the rules of the school, are examined in an attempt to integrate the hidden and explicit curriculums. For example, if the explicit curriculum articulates the importance of democratic procedures and due process, the school's rules should be directed toward the principle of fairness. Students, depending on their developmental level, would also be involved in the processes of curriculum building and shaping the school's rule structure.

Kohlberg has conducted research on the effects of a community-school focus. In Israel, interviews were conducted at a collective settlement, and the results were compared with interviews of a group of disadvantaged adolescents in an inner city in the United States. Kohlberg and his associates found that a substantial proportion of the inner-city group were at stages 1 and 2. At the kibbutz school, however, none of the students was at this level. Most were at the conventional level and a few were at the post-conventional level.[38]

The Teacher's Role

The teacher is a stimulator of moral development. He does not attempt to accelerate development but tries to prevent stage retardation. The teacher is warm and supportive in order to develop an open atmosphere where ideas can be shared. However, the teacher also confronts the students with contradictions and inadequacies in their thinking. He attempts to be just and fair in classroom-management procedures.

Applicability of the Model

Its moderate structure and sound theoretical perspective encourage wide use of this model. Materials have also been developed so that it can be used at most levels and in many subject areas. Some teachers complain, however, that students get bored with moral dilemmas. If the conflicts presented are not genuine or meaningful to the students, the discussion can become a mere game to the students.

The Learning Environment

Kohlberg's model of moral development is nurturant. The teacher does not directly instruct the student in moral reasoning but creates an environment that facilitates moral development.

SUMMARY: DEVELOPMENTAL MODELS

	Ego Development	Psychosocial Development	Psychological Education	Moral Development
Aims	Effective resolution of stage crises	Eventual realization of independence in learning	Realization of personal identity and autonomy as well as the ability to relate to and communicate with other people	Avoidance of stage retardation and eventual attainment of post-conventional reasoning
Teaching Process	1. Identify stage of development 2. Match activities to stage of development	1. Identify stage 2. Match activities to stage of development 3. Assess outcomes	1. Exposing student to basic concepts of human development 2. Creating laboratory situation for student role experimentation	1. Identify the child's stage of development 2. Present developmentally related moral dilemmas for discussion 3. In discussing the dilemma, provide a context where the student is exposed to reasoning one stage higher than his own level 4. Assist the child in working through the contradictions in his reasoning
Teacher's Role	Maintain personal authenticity and not to accept negative student identity	Recognize student needs and relate activities to those needs	a) Relate laboratory experiences to concepts of human development b) Be flexible and cooperative with other staff members in team effort	Create an open atmosphere for discussion, yet also probe the student for inadequacies in reasoning
Amount of Structure	Moderate	High to Moderate	Moderate to Low	Moderate

Figure 4

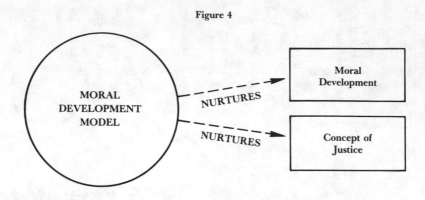

Notes

1. Lawrence Kohlberg, "Humanistic and Cognitive-Developmental Perspectives on Psychological Education," in *Curriculum and Cultural Change*, edited by R. E. Purpel and M. Belanger (Berkeley, Calif.: McCutchan, 1972), pp. 394–402.
2. Erik H. Erikson, *Childhood and Society* (New York: Norton, 1950), p. 222.
3. Ibid., pp. 209–11.
4. Ibid., p. 211.
5. Robert Coles, *Erik Erikson: The Growth of His Work* (Boston: Little, Brown, 1970), pp. 18–19.
6. Lillian Weber, *The English Infant School and Informal Education* (Englewood Cliffs, N.J.: Prentice-Hall, 1971).
7. Joseph Featherstone, *Schools Where Children Learn* (New York: Liveright, 1971).
8. Erik H. Erikson, *Identity: Youth and Crisis* (New York: Norton, 1968).
9. Coles, p. 157.
10. See John P. Miller, "Schooling and Self-Alienation: A Conceptual View," *Journal of Educational Thought* 7 (1973): 105–20.
11. Ralph Mosher and Norman Sprinthall et al., "Psychological Education: A Means to Promote Personal Development During Adolescence," in *Curriculum and the Cultural Revolution*, edited by R. E. Purpel and M. Belanger (Berkeley, Calif.: McCutchan, 1972), p. 300.
12. Mosher and Sprinthall, "Psychological Education in the Secondary Schools," *American Psychologist* 25 (1970): 915.
13. Ibid., p. 919.
14. Mosher and Sprinthall, "Psychological Education: A Means to Promote Personal Development During Adolescence," pp. 359–60.
15. Ibid., p. 363.
16. Mosher and Sprinthall, "Psychological Education in Secondary Schools," p. 920.
17. Ibid.
18. Mosher and Sprinthall, "Psychological Education: A Means to Promote Development During Adolescence," pp. 323–35.
19. Alan J. Hoffman and Thomas Ryan, *Social Studies and the Child's Expanding Self* (New York: Intext Press, 1973), p. 14.

20. Ibid., p. 20.
21. Ibid., p. 16.
22. Ibid., p. 166.
23. Ibid., pp. 166–67.
24. Ibid., p. 192.
25. Lawrence Kohlberg and Elliott Turiel, "Moral Development and Moral Education" in *Psychology and Educational Practices,* edited by G. Lesser (New York: Scott, Foresman, 1971), pp. 413–14.
26. Lawrence Kohlberg, "Stages of Moral Development as a Basis for Moral Education," in *Moral Education: Interdisciplinary Approaches,* edited by C. M. Beck, B. S. Crittenden, and E. Sullivan (Toronto: University of Toronto Press, 1971), pp. 86–88.
27. Kohlberg and Turiel, "Moral Development and Moral Education," p. 448.
28. Ibid., p. 434.
29. Ibid.
30. Ibid., p. 435.
31. Ibid.
32. Ibid.
33. Ibid., p. 436.
34. Ibid.
35. Lawrence Kohlberg, "Continuities and Discontinuities in Childhood and Adult Moral Development Revisited," in *Life Span Developmental Psychology: Research and Theory,* edited by Baltes and Schail (New York: Academic Press; in press).
36. Kohlberg, "Stages of Moral Development as a Basis for Moral Education," p. 44.
37. Ibid., p. 50.
38. Kohlberg and Turiel, p. 449.

OTHER MODELS AND BIBLIOGRAPHY

Other Models

Role Taking—A Developmental Model

Robert Selman has studied how the child moves from egocentric thought to sociocentric thought through different role-taking stages. His ideas are relevant to Kohlberg's work and to the Shaftels' role-playing model. See Robert Selman, "The Development of Socio-Cognitive Understanding: A Guide to Educational and Clinical Practice," in *Morality: Theory, Research and Social Issues,* edited by Thomas Lickona (New York: Holt, Rinehart & Winston, 1975).

Bibliography

Coles, Robert. *Erik Erikson: The Growth of His Work.* Boston: Little,

Brown, 1970. This excellent summary of Erikson's work presents his theory in a clear and illuminating manner.

Erikson, Erik H. "Play and Actuality," in *Play and Development,* edited by Maria Piers. New York: Norton, 1972. Erikson explains his thoughts on play in relation to developmental theory.

————. *Childhood and Society.* New York: Norton, 1950.

————. *Identity: Youth and Crisis.* New York: Norton, 1968. This and the preceding text contain the essentials of his developmental theory.

Hoffman, Alan J., and Ryan, Thomas F. *Social Studies and the Child's Expanding Self.* New York: Intext Press, 1973. Developmental theory and a large number of classroom activities are presented. Despite conceptual problems, this is an interesting and practical text for teachers.

Kohlberg, Lawrence. *Collected Papers on Moral Development and Moral Education.* Cambridge, Mass.: Harvard Graduate School of Education, Spring 1973. An excellent collection of Kohlberg's papers. The emphasis is theoretical, but practical applications are also discussed.

Mosher, Ralph, and Sprinthall, Norman. "Psychological Education in the Secondary Schools," *American Psychologist* 25 (1970): 911–24.

————. "Psychological Education: A Means to Promote Personal Development During Adolescence," in *Curriculum and the Cultural Revolution,* edited by R. E. Purpel and M. Belanger. Berkeley, Calif.: McCutchan, 1972. These two articles present an overview of the theory and practice of psychological education. The latter article describes in detail various laboratory activities in psychological education.

CHAPTER 4
SELF-CONCEPT MODELS

The five teaching models in this chapter focus on identity. Developing an identity or self-concept means finding out what you ultimately value and how to live in a manner that reflects those values. The psychologist William James described an authentic sense of identity as follows:

> A man's character is discernible in the mental or moral attitude in which, when it came upon him, he felt himself most deeply and intensely active and alive. At such moments there is a voice inside which speaks and says: "This is the real me!"
>
> Such experience always includes . . . an element of active tension, of holding my own, as it were, and trusting outward things to perform their part so as to make it a full harmony, but without any guaranty that they will. Make it a guaranty . . . and the attitude immediately becomes to my consciousness stagnant and stingless. Take away the guaranty, and I feel a sort of deep enthusiastic bliss, of bitter willingness to do and suffer anything . . . and which, although it is a mere mood or emotion to which I can give no form in words, authenticates itself to me as the deepest principle of all active and theoretic determination which I possess. . . .[1]

In sum, the aim of the self-concept models is to put the student in touch with himself so that he can direct and guide his own behavior without constant reference to the expectations of others.

The *values clarification model* facilitates the student's ability to clarify values, which are integral to self-concept. For example, a

49

person who commits himself to the value of conservation and to acting on that commitment develops an identity that is associated with conservation and ecology.

Gerald Weinstein and Mario Fantini have developed a teaching model that focuses on *identity education*. It contains a number of steps that involve ascertaining student concerns, diagnosing them, and developing content vehicles, learning skills, and teaching procedures that are congruent with them. It asks the teacher to employ an ongoing process of curriculum development in order to facilitate a positive self-concept in students.

The *classroom meeting model* facilitates identity development by involving the student in responsible decision making. In relation to his own social behavior, the student sets values and commits himself to those values. The teacher and the group support and reinforce the student in his commitment.

The *role playing model* developed by the Shaftels is conducive to both self-concept development and group interaction. It is placed in the self-concept family because such theorists as Kohlberg and Erikson have suggested that role playing is integral to the development of autonomous selfhood.

Carl Rogers' *self-directed model* supports the development of the fully functioning person who is in touch with his feelings and concerns. It puts responsibility for this development on the student himself.

The models in this chapter range from high to low in structure and thus offer strategies for a variety of teaching circumstances. Teachers working with students at the lower conceptual levels will find the values clarification model useful. The identity education, classroom meeting, and role-playing models present learning environments for the student at the moderate CL stages. The self-directed model, with its unstructured approach, is appropriate for students at higher conceptual levels.

VALUES CLARIFICATION

Theoretical Orientation

Should I wear clothes that I like or that my parents want me to wear?

Should I smoke marijuana just because some of my friends do?

What do I enjoy most in life, and what does this tell me about myself?

How much time should I spend watching TV?

According to Sidney Simon and his associates, these questions are just a few of the issues faced by young people that lend themselves to values clarification. Some of the other relevant areas are "politics, religion, work-leisure time, school, sex, family, material possessions, culture (art, music, literature), friends, money, aging, death, race, war-peace, and rules."[2] The values clarification approach helps young people to examine these areas, clarify the value issues involved, and develop their own value systems with respect to the issues. The approach does not attempt to impose a particular set of values but allows the student to clarify his own position. The process of valuing, according to Simon and Louis Raths, consists of seven subprocesses:[3]

1. *Choosing freely.* If an individual is coerced to adopt a particular value, there is little likelihood that he will consciously integrate that value into his value structure.

2. *Choosing from alternatives.* This is closely related to the first subprocess. Making a number of alternatives available to the individual increases the probability that the individual can choose freely.

3. *Choosing after considering the consequences.* Valuing is a thoughtful process in which the individual attempts consciously to predict what will happen if he chooses a particular value. Choosing impulsively will not lead to an intelligent value system.

4. *Prizing and cherishing.* According to Simon and Raths, we should respect our values and consider them an integral aspect of our existence.

5. *Affirming.* If we have chosen our values freely after considering the consequences, then we should be willing to affirm these values publicly. We should not be ashamed of our values but should be willing to share them when the occasion arises.

6. *Acting upon choices.* The values we hold should be apparent from our actions. In fact, the way we spend our time should reflect the values we cherish.

7. *Repeating.* If we act on our values we should do so in a consistent and repetitive pattern. If our actions are inconsistent with our values, then we should examine more closely the relationship between our values and actions.

Classroom Applications

In the book *Values Clarification,* Simon and his associates present seventy-nine classroom activities for values education, each designed to facilitate a different subprocess of valuing. The three strategies discussed below represent the basic phases of values clarification: prizing, choosing, and acting.

One of the most popular strategies, called "Twenty Things You Love to Do," involves *prizing.* The teacher asks the students to list the twenty activities they most like to do. These can include anything from reading comics to going on a trip and can be important aspects of life or simple daily routines. After the lists are completed, Simon suggests that the students place beside each activity certain symbols which will be self-revealing. For example:

1. "Use the letter *R* for those things which have an element of risk. This can be physical risk, emotional risk, or intellectual risk."[4]
2. Put *N5* next to "those items which you would not have listed five years ago."[5] This can indicate how much some personal values have changed.
3. Put *F* beside those activities that your father does. This can indicate that some values are shared with father and some values differ.
4. Use the letter *P* for the activities that you would publicly affirm.

After completing the lists, the students can share their activities with other students or the entire class. Eventually the teacher should read from his own list. As in most values clarification activities, the teacher should be able to convey his own values openly, although not too early in the process.

Another strategy focuses on *choosing* among competing alternative values. This is the *forced-choice ladder.* Here the teacher asks the students to construct a choice ladder with eight steps. The teacher then presents a series of alternatives which represent certain values. Using a key word, a student ranks each alternative depending on how strongly he feels about a specific value, or on the basis of whether he is for or against the value. As an example of the latter, the student would rank eight items ranging from "the person I'd least like to be like" at the bottom of the ladder, to "the person I'd most like to be like" at the top.

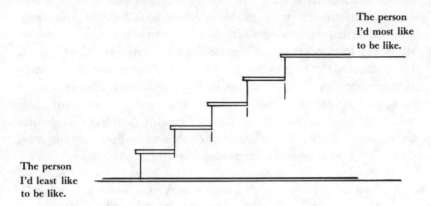

The person
I'd most like
to be like.

The person
I'd least like
to be like.

A set of choices that could be used in this ladder is as follows:

1. A rich person who gives very generously to charities. (*Philanthropist*)
2. A person whose prime concern is conserving the environment so that he becomes involved in various conservation projects. (*Ecologist*)
3. An individual whose main concern in life is integrating himself through self-help techniques, such as meditation and yoga. (*Meditator*)
4. An individual whose main focus in life is getting involved with and helping other people through the Salvation Army. (*Helper*)
5. An individual whose main value is serving his country through the armed forces. (*Patriot*)
6. A person whose primary focus in life is his small business. He devotes most of his energy toward running an efficient and profitable business. (*Business person*)
7. An individual whose primary concern is taking care of and spending time with his family. (*Family head*)
8. A person who feels that the only hope for humanity is through world organizations and who commits his life to working for the World Federalists. (*Internationalist*)

After completing their ladders, students can get together and compare their lists. This can lead to a discussion of the reasons behind each student's choices and provide an opportunity to clarify the students' reasoning with regard to their values.

A third strategy involves the *acting* phase of the valuing process. Students learn to consider alternatives for action in various situations and to make their actions congruent with their values. Here the student is presented with a situation that calls for some proposed action. The teacher asks that each student decide what he or she would do in the situation. The students can write their solutions and compare them in small groups. Simon suggests that they discuss their proposals and try to decide which are the most desirable. Some possible situations include:

1. You are walking behind someone. You see him take out a cigarette pack, withdraw the last cigarette, and put it in his mouth, crumple the package, and nonchalantly toss it over his shoulder onto the sidewalk. You are 25 feet behind him. Ideally, what would you do?[6]

2. You're driving on a two-lane road behind another car. You notice that one of its wheels is wobbling more and more. It looks as if the nuts are coming off one by one. There's no way to pass the driver, because cars are coming in the other direction in a steady stream. What would you do?[7]

3. You are driving along the highway alone on a rainy day. In front of you is a hitchhiker dressed in hippie garb holding a sign lettered with the name of your destination. What would you do?

The Teacher's Role

The values clarification strategies contain a number of highly structured activities that would be appropriate for students at a low CL level. They can be also used with students at a high CL level but seem best for teachers looking for identity-facilitating activities with a good deal of structure.

The teacher should be prepared to accept different student values without being judgmental. He should not permit students to "put down" other students during the sharing of values. He should not only listen to and accept their values, but should also be willing to offer his own. If he attempts to conceal his own views, an atmosphere conducive to interchange and growth will not develop. This does not mean that the teacher should moralize, however. He states his position without imposing it on others. The teacher should also allow a student who doesn't want to participate to "pass." The idea is not to put excessive pressure on students but to create an atmosphere in which all will want to participate.

Applicability of the Model

This has been a popular model with teachers. Because the approach is structured and easily applied to the classroom, teachers can quickly integrate it into their curriculum. Some teachers report dramatic and encouraging changes in students after using the strategies.

However, some of the approaches are simplistic. For example, having the students vote on whether they enjoy watching movies or playing cards doesn't seem to be a particularly enlightening exercise.[8] The teacher should examine each exercise carefully before trying it so that its maximum value can be realized.

The theoretical framework has also been criticized. In fact, Howard Kirschenbaum, an associate of Simon, has pointed out inadequacies in the seven subprocesses of valuing and has offered an alternative framework that includes feeling, thinking, and communicating as well as choosing and acting in the valuing process.[9]

The Learning Environment

The values clarification model attempts to instruct the student in a certain valuing process through structured strategies. Many of the strategies (e.g. forced-choice ladder, values voting) present situations in which the student chooses values. Other strategies focus on prizing and acting consistently. The model also nurtures respect for values held by others.

IDENTITY EDUCATION

Gerald Weinstein and Mario Fantini have developed a model for Identity Education. Central to this model is a process of curriculum development built around the concerns of the learner. The focus of their teaching model therefore involves ascertaining

Figure 5

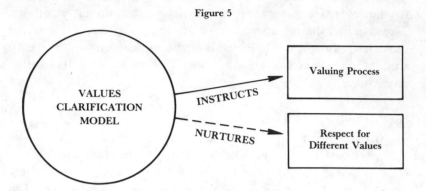

and diagnosing learner concerns and then building lessons around those concerns. Weinstein and Fantini also attempt to integrate the affective and cognitive spheres in their curriculum.

Although specific objectives for the "curriculum of affect" depend on the particular student group, they often focus on three consistent themes: a desire for a positive self-image, a wish to establish connections with others and society at large, and a desire to gain control over one's life. Thus, the broad goals for identity education are a positive identity, a sense of relatedness, and self-determination.

Theoretical Application

This teaching model is based on several steps and has been diagramed as follows:[10]

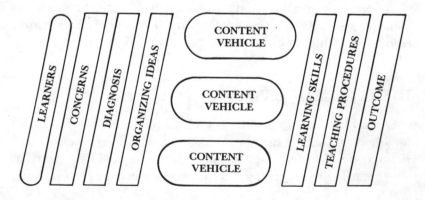

The first step involves identifying the learners. This means assessing the following characteristics, among others: "developmental (age), economic (lower, middle, or upper income), geographic (rural or urban), cultural and racial or ethnic characteristics."[11] This first step centers on the characteristics common to the group rather than focusing initially on the individual student.

The second and third steps involve ascertaining the learners' concerns and diagnosing the reasons for these concerns. A concern connotes an inner uneasiness for the individual and is deeper and more pervasive than a simple interest or feeling. Students' concerns often center around such issues as self-image and disconnectedness. Concerns can be identified through what learners say and write about themselves. Through diagnosis, the third step, the teacher attempts to develop ideas about teaching strategies that can meet those concerns. This means looking behind the student's statement. For instance, the statement, "It's no use trying, there's nothing you can do about it" made by a middle-class child might mean that he lives in an overprotected situation, while the same statement by a lower-class student could indicate a lack of protection and support. Thus the same statement can lead to different teaching strategies depending on the student who made the statement.[12]

Weinstein and Fantini describe several activities that can facilitate the diagnostic process. "Faraway Island," for example, is designed to uncover students' self-perceptions and value systems.[13] The following instructions are used to introduce this exercise to children:

> Assume that you have to spend the rest of your life on a remote island with just six people and no one else. Imagine that! None of these six people can be anyone you already know, but you're allowed to specify what they should be like. What kinds of people would you pick to live the rest of your life with? You might think about how old they'd be, their sex, the things they'd like to do and the things they wouldn't like to do, their personalities, their looks, or any other qualities. Assume, also, that all your basic needs are taken care of, so you don't have to scrounge around for food, clothing, and shelter. All you have to do is describe as fully as you can what the people you'd choose to live with would be like.

The responses of a racially mixed group of 15- and 16-year-olds enrolled in an Upward Bound project in New Jersey included the following:

> FIRST GIRL: First I'd pick a doctor in case I get sick. It could be anybody, as long as they're nice and can be trusted. Just as long as I have the doctor first. . . .
>
> FIRST BOY: Well, they'd all have to be working because they'd all have to come up with an equal amount of rent, you know. So I would pick people that know what they're talking about and not no dumb person . . . you know, you're talking about certain subjects and they're wandering. I would get six people same as Victor, his personality and everything, his actions and like that.
>
> LEADER: Anybody else?
>
> FIRST BOY: I would like one or two people that's older than I. Can't be anybody I know. I would like a person like a college professor that's hip. He knows what's happening and all, and you know he's smart, and he could keep order in case anything happens, you know. Let's say two older people, two girls, in the same age bracket, understanding, and what not. And then another guy around my age. And I would like these to possess qualities and be able to do things. Maybe one is musically inclined and has talent and you could do this. And another one draws, you know, things that would keep you busy.
>
> SECOND BOY: I would like to have one older guy that's real smart. . . . He'd picka part and argue like mad. You couldn't put nothing over on him. And I'd like a guy and a girl around my age that I could talk with that would be good conversations . . . .

Weinstein and Fantini found that these students tended to select people who had the greatest control over their lives, indicating that self-determination was a basic concern. They also were concerned with economic security and racial segregation. The diagnostic techniques generate student data related to identity questions. They can help the teacher "read" student needs more accurately and then shape activities to meet some of these needs.

Once the teacher has made a diagnosis he can develop a set of behavioral outcomes aimed at meeting some of these concerns. For example, if the concern is a more positive self-image, the

teachers would look for behavioral indicators that a more positive identity is developing. Sometimes student statements can be
indicative of change in self-concept.

A fifth step involves developing a theme to organize the lesson.
The organizing idea or theme gives direction and coherence to
teaching. It is essential that the theme be relevant to student
concerns. Examples of some organizing ideas include:

1. **You use people, things, and events to tell you who you are.**
2. **Some people, things, and events are more important to you
   than others.**
3. **The most important ones are those you use most often in
   judging yourself.**
4. **It is important to know what you are using to measure your
   own self-worth.**
5. **Certain things, people, and events are important to you because of (a) where you live and who else lives there, (b) what
   you think is good for people, and (c) the fact that you are
   you.**[14]

After the selection of an organizing idea, the teacher selects
content vehicles to achieve the desired outcomes. Several avenues
are open to the teacher, including subject disciplines, different
media, and excursions. The teacher should not overlook the students' concerns, feelings, and experiences as content vehicles.
These are vital to identity education.

Learning skills are also part of the model and include skills
that the student needs in order to deal with the content vehicles—for example, basic skills such as reading and writing; learning-to-learn skills such as problem-solving skills and other process
skills needed to deal with information and concepts; and self-
awareness skills that focus on the ability to be more in touch with
oneself and more effective in communicating emotional states.

Teaching strategies are then developed appropriate to the
learning skills, content vehicles, organizing ideas, and outcomes.
Weinstein and Fantini feel that it is important to match procedures to the learning styles of the students.

Finally, the teacher should attempt to evaluate the effect of the
curriculum, asking such questions as "Has the children's behavior changed? Were the content vehicles the best that could have

been employed? Were the cognitive skills and teacher procedures the most effective for achieving the affective goals?"[15]

Classroom Application

The following example, from *Toward Humanistic Education*, shows the model in action.

THE LEARNERS

The learners were inner-city children, aged seven to nine, whose families had an annual income of $3,000 or less. Most of the children were Negro, but there was a sprinkling of white and Indian children who lived on the fringes of the Negro ghetto.

CONCERNS

The children's major concerns, identified through observation, centered on self-rejection, disconnectedness, and powerlessness.

Clues indicating self-rejection included the following statements.

—"The kids are always calling me a black monkey."

—"I do not like my name."

—"I'm one of those disadvantaged kids."

—"I can't do this work. That's why I'm in this slow class."

—"I wish I were a man."

Clues indicating disconnectedness, reflecting the children's concern for connection with one another or with society at large, included:

—"You can't trust nobody, white or Negro."

—"I'm not really accepted by white people because of my color or by Negroes because I think different than they do."

Clues indicating powerlessness, the children's concern for greater control over their destiny, included:

"It's no use trying, there's nothing you can do."

"The principal runs the school and the student council, and he doesn't want to know what our problems are."

"So what if I get an education? That doesn't mean I can get a job."

BEHAVIORAL OUTCOMES

The primary aim of this unit was to help students to develop a more positive self-concept; the other two concerns were touched on only tangentially. The behavioral objective, therefore, was to help each child to

1. realize that his personality is a composite of many kinds of behavior, and that these behaviors are determined;
2. identify at least two ways in which he is special, citing his own special characteristics;
3. discover and remark upon the universality of his feelings;
4. analyze his likes and dislikes and compare them with the likes and dislikes of his peers.

ORGANIZERS

The following organizers served to integrate concerns, desired outcomes, and teaching procedures.
1. Everyone is very special.
2. There are many subselves that make up the self.
3. Everyone has feelings that are distinctly his own, but there are many situations in which people share the same feelings.

CONTENT VEHICLES AND TEACHING PROCEDURES

Two major content vehicles were employed. The first was the book *Who Are You?* by Joan and Roger Bradfield, which the teacher read aloud in its entirety at the beginning of the unit. The second was a personal folder which each of the students constructed and contributed to in the course of the unit.

EPISODES 1 AND 2. The purpose of these "episodes" was to show some of the ways in which children differ from one another. The teacher read the book aloud and then engaged the students in discussion. His first questions related to physical characteristics.

Teacher: What makes you special among everyone else in the room? Are you different in size, looks, and so on? (*He used the categories presented in the book.*)
—What kinds of things do you like? Why?
—What kinds of people do you like? Why?
—What are these people like?
—What people are important to you?
—To whom are you important?
The teacher then asked each student to draw a self-portrait showing that he was different from everyone else. He suggested that the picture show something special about the student himself or something that he liked or did. The children added explanatory comments to their drawings. A photograph of each child was placed in his folder, facing the drawing.

EPISODE 3. The purpose of this episode was to make the children aware of their feelings.

Teacher: What kinds of things make us happy? Why?

—Can some things make us happy sometimes and sad at other times? What kind of things?

—What people make us happy? Do they make us happy all the time?

—Are there times when we can change things that make us happy or sad? How?

—Let's draw a picture of something that makes us happy.

—Let's write a sentence about something that makes us happy.

The completed booklets were shown to other classes, to the principal, and, most important of all, to parents, who were invited to come to the school to see them. The teacher pointed out that the booklet could be thought of as analogous to the person, or "big me," which depends on and is made up of many parts—the "little me's." Subsequent lessons were used to reinforce the concept of "me."

LEARNING SKILLS

Some basic skills were needed for working with the concepts and content vehicles pointing to the desired outcomes: the ability to write a complete thought, and the ability to listen to, and take part in, discussion. They were practiced before introducing the lessons.

Learning-to-learn skills, on the other hand, were developed during the lessons themselves. The ability to generate alternative solutions is one such skill. When the teacher asked such questions as "Are there times when we can change things that make us happy or sad?" he was furnishing practice in this skill. The ability to negotiate with people who have different points of view is another learning-to-learn skill. Role-playing provided an opportunity to develop this skill.[16]

The Teacher's Role

The teacher should be capable of diagnosing and dealing openly with student concerns. He should convey a genuine empathy with students. It is also important that the teacher integrate affective concerns with learning skills and not isolate the curriculum of affect from the cognitive curriculum.

The exercises run from high to moderate in structure, with

most in the moderate range. They are appropriate for students at low to moderate CL stages.

Applicability of the Model

This model seems to be applicable to a variety of situations, since it is open-ended and dependent on student concerns. The key is for the teacher to use the curriculum-development process to generate his own set of outcomes, content vehicles, and teaching procedures.

A number of strategies were developed by Weinstein and Fantini specifically for the disadvantaged child, but these can be used with other children as well. The balance between structure and open-endedness makes the model popular with teachers who are interested in self-concept education. However, it is also a demanding approach, since the teacher must be able to diagnose student concerns and develop strategies based on these concerns.

The Learning Environment

The identity education model is both instructional and nurturant. It instructs the student in basic learning skills and nurtures a positive self-image, self-control, and connectedness to others.

Figure 6

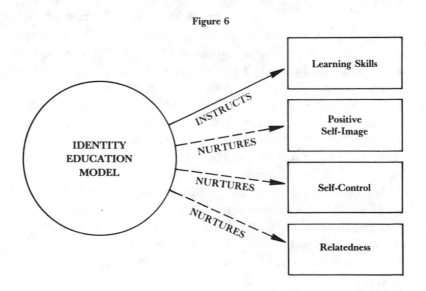

CLASSROOM MEETING MODEL

Theoretical Orientation

William Glasser, a psychiatrist, argues that all humans have two basic emotional needs: love and self-worth. Unless these needs are met the individual cannot gain a sense of identity.

> **Love and self-worth are so intertwined that they may properly be related through the use of the term *identity*. Thus we may say that the single basic need that people have is the requirement for an identity: the belief that we are someone in distinction to others, and that the someone is important and worthwhile. Then *love and self-worth may be considered the two pathways* that mankind has discovered lead to a successful identity. People able to develop a successful identity are those who have learned to find their way through the two pathways of love and self-worth, the latter dependent upon knowledge and the ability to solve the problems of life successfully.[17]**

Schools traditionally have been more concerned with meeting students' need to feel worthwhile by imparting knowledge and fostering the ability to think. However, Glasser reports, because of the breakdown of so many families, teachers now are "overwhelmed with children who need affection, but do not know how to react to the obvious need for love of many of their students."[18]

The teacher's task, then, is to respond to the students' need for identity. The first step is teacher involvement. The teacher must convey respect for the child's worth and must also create an atmosphere in which other students can share in this involvement. It should be evident to the students that the teacher *cares* about them and their basic concerns. Second, the teacher's involvement should concern current problems. To break the cycle of failure that entraps some children, Glasser suggests that the teacher focus on present behavior rather than past problems because the child can deal with the present more effectively. Third, Glasser points out that the teacher should focus predominantly on behavior, since responding only to the child's feelings and ignoring his behavior can lead to his continued failure.

Fourth, the teacher should encourage the students to make personal value judgments about their behavior. After the children have made a value judgment, the teacher should not manipulate the world to protect them from the consequences of their behavior. The teacher should also point out the consequences of the students' value positions so that they can reflect on their value commitments. However, the teacher should not accept failing behavior. "No matter how often [the child] fails, he should again and again be asked for a value judgment until he begins to doubt that what he is defending is really the best for him."[19]

Once the child makes a value judgment about his behavior, he can then make a commitment to act in accordance with the values he has selected. If, for example, the child makes the judgment that interrupting the class is undesirable behavior, he must commit himself to a course of action that is conducive to his learning as well as his classmates' learning.

Finally, after the child has chosen and committed himself to a set of values, the teacher creates a situation where the child follows through with the course of action he has selected. No excuse is acceptable for not following through. This course of action suggested by Glasser substitutes self-discipline for punishment.

> The teacher must then ask, in words appropriate to the age of the child and to the situation, whether his behavior is helping him, her, the class, or the school. If the child says, "No, what I am doing is not helping," the teacher must then ask the child what he could do that is different. This is exactly the opposite of what happens in almost all schools and homes when a child misbehaves. Ordinarily, the teacher or parent tells the child that he is doing wrong and that if he doesn't change he'll be punished. This traditional but ineffective approach removes the responsibility for his bad behavior from the child. The teacher makes the judgment and enforces the punishment; the child has little responsibility for what happens.[20]

Classroom Applications

The mechanism for realizing the goals described above is the classroom meeting model. In this type of meeting the focus is on creating a framework where students can make value judgments about their behavior and then commit themselves to a course of action that reflects those values. There are six steps to the model: (1) creating a climate of involvement; (2) exposing the problem for discussion; (3) making a personal value judgment; (4) identifying alternative courses of action; (5) making a commitment; and (6) behavioral follow-up.

Glasser illustrates these phases in action in his book *Schools Without Failures* by describing a *social-problem-solving meeting* in an eighth-grade class dealing with truancy. Since Glasser was new to the class, he could not create a real climate of involvement, which requires a longer-term relationship and a nonjudgmental atmosphere. In this situation Glasser tried to have the students think about their own reasons for cutting school and about how they might help the class improve its attendance record.

Glasser started the discussion by asking if everyone was present that day. The students indicated that eight of their classmates were not there, and some even admitted that they had skipped class in the past. This led to a discussion of the reasons for their truancy. Thus the initial phase of the meeting involved exposing the problem for open, honest discussion. (In this example, the teacher opened the discussion, but a student can also raise an issue for a social-problem-solving meeting.)

Next, Glasser tried to get the students to make a judgment about the value of attendance. Glasser's example is somewhat weak at this point, because the students did not have a free choice among alternatives. Instead, Glasser pressed the students toward what he felt was a reasonable value—attending school. He then attempted to get the students to sign a statement that they would come to school the next day. About one-third were willing to sign the statement and the rest refused. Glasser then asked the nonsigners, "If you won't sign a paper stating you will come tomorrow, will you sign a paper stating that you won't sign a paper?"[21] Another third of the class was willing to sign this paper, and the remaining students refused to sign anything. This phase of the meeting, of course, constituted the fifth step of making a commitment. Since Glasser was invited to the school for only the one day, there was no chance for behavioral follow-up. Under normal circumstances the teacher would check with the students to see whether they were living up to their commitments.

The second type of meeting described by Glasser is the *open-ended meeting*. This is intended for discussion of any "thought-provoking question related to [the students'] lives—questions that may also be related to the curriculum of the classroom."[22] The focus here is not on factual questions but on trying to stimulate the child to think and relate to broader curriculum-related questions. Note that the focus is more academic here than in the social-problem-solving meeting. Glasser suggests that the open-ended meeting can be started with the question "What is interesting to you?" Glasser lists other questions that are useful in starting a meeting—for example, on the topic of boredom:

> **If schools were eliminated completely, how would you spend your time?**
> **Would you be bored?**
> **What is boredom? How would you explain it?**
> **What are some of the times when you have been most bored in your whole life?**
> **What are some of the things that most interest you?**
> **Are all children bored?**
> **What is the difference between the people who are bored a lot and those who are not?**
> **Is school work always boring?**
> **Is there some school work that is never boring?**
> **How would you suggest that school work be made less boring?**[23]

The *educational diagnostic meeting,* the third type discussed by Glasser, focuses on finding out where the class "is at" with respect to a particular problem in order to gauge how effective the teacher's instruction has been. Glasser discusses an example of students studying the U.S. Constitution. After the diagnostic meeting it was obvious to the teacher that the class had no real understanding of the Constitution and its principles. This indicated to the teacher that he needed to re-examine his teaching approach to the Constitution.[24]

Many teachers are probably familiar with one or more of Glasser's meetings and may even be using them without referring to them as "meetings." Glasser urges that the teacher move toward a situation where all activities have the involvement and openness of the meeting so that meetings lose their special status. In short, the entire school day can become a classroom meeting.

The Teacher's Role

The teacher should be warm and supportive, yet he should press the child to make value judgments and commitments. The teacher creates a situation in which the child becomes responsible for his own behavior and thus gains a sense of identity.

Glasser also makes a number of suggestions for holding classroom meetings. With regard to the social-problem-solving meeting, Glasser advises that the focus be on solutions and not on fault-finding. The meetings should also avoid repetition and dealing constantly with the problems of one or two students. There should be no interruption to correct bad grammar or speech in the social-problem-solving meeting, since the focus is on broader problems.

As for the mechanics of the meetings, Glasser feels a circle with chairs close together is the most effective spatial arrangement; that 10 to 30 minutes is an adequate time limit for the lower grades and 30 to 45 minutes for children in the intermediate division; that hand raising is necessary in order to avoid having too many students speak at once; and that teachers should feel free to adopt a team approach to leadership of the meetings. Teachers can give each other feedback and suggestions for conducting effective meetings.[25]

Applicability of the Model

This model has wide applicability. It is generally moderate in structure but could even be varied in structure since it is flexible in format. The teacher does not require special training but must be committed to involvement with the students.

I feel that the teacher must be careful to let the child make the personal value judgment. It would be possible in this approach for the teacher to impose a particular value rather than letting the child freely choose his own set of values.

Figure 7

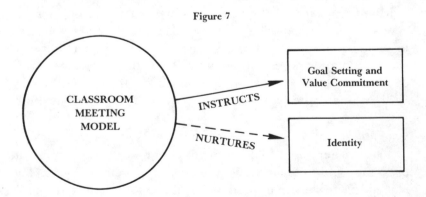

The Learning Environment

As a learning environment the classroom meeting model instructs and nurtures. It nurtures a sense of identity and instructs the student to set goals and commit himself to the goals and values he has chosen.

ROLE PLAYING

Theoretical Orientation

Fannie and George Shaftel have developed a model of teaching from role playing through their book *Role Playing for Social Values,* which details a rationale and a teaching process for enactment. Their model might easily fit within the self-concept and group-orientation models. In fact, the Shaftels argue that the major functions of role playing are to help "the individual child to become 'inner directed' at the same time that he learns to live well in groups."[26] In terms of "inner-directed" development, the Shaftels suggest that role playing can improve the child's self-concept, since the teacher can give a student opportunities to engage in roles different from those designated by his peers. Sometimes a child is slotted into a fixed role by his classmates. The teacher, however, can develop situations in which an "undervalued child" can demonstrate skills and qualities not perceived by his peers. Role playing can thus provide the student with a different status as well as a new possibility of recognition. The Shaftels conclude:

> We have some initial, empirical evidence to support the belief that the teacher, by carefully selecting roles for an underappreciated individual to play, over the period of a planned sequence of role-playing sessions, can do much to help him win respect and sometimes even admiration from the classroom group; and, thereby, to help him acquire a higher degree of self-respect and confidence.[27]

Self-concept is also enhanced if the student is given the opportunity to explore different situations and examine his own reactions to them. Thus, he grows in self-concept as he becomes comfortable in a variety of roles. Rapid social change also requires that the person adapt to different roles within his basic framework of inner-directed values. Through role playing the individual can practice roles that he may have to assume during his development.

Role playing also can facilitate inner-directedness through clarification of the individual's values and beliefs. Each role-playing situation presents a range of values to be explored and examined. Gradually the student can clarify his own value position through these experiences.

> **As children participate in role-playing sessions, each one has an opportunity to propose, through his role-playing and in the discussions that follow enactments, his own ways of solving human relations problems. Often his proposals are spontaneous and based on unconsciously held values. In the discussions following an enactment, and in the demonstration of next steps (or consequences) that may occur in further enactments, the teacher-leader, with the help of the child's reacting peers, may guide him to consciously face his choices. In this way he is helped to become aware of his values and, in a positive group climate, he can explore the effects of various choices upon himself and others.[28]**

Other positive results of role playing, according to the Shaftels, are described below.

SENSITIVITY TO THE FEELINGS OF OTHERS.   In role playing the student can feel how it is to be in certain situations and thus develop empathy for other people who are in similar circumstances.

RELEASE OF TENSIONS AND FEELINGS.   It is sometimes helpful to a student to act out his feelings concerning a certain situation and realize that other students share these feelings.

DIAGNOSIS OF THE NEEDS OF CHILDREN.   The way the child behaves in various situations can be revealing to the teacher, to fellow students, and to the student himself. Certain social needs (e.g., the need for recognition) can be assessed and situations developed to deal with these needs.

EXPLORING THE VALUES OF ONE'S CULTURE AND DIFFERENT SUB-CULTURES.   Role playing can allow an individual to examine various aspects of his culture. For example, the democratic process can be examined through role-playing situations.

IMPROVEMENT OF THE SOCIAL STRUCTURE AND VALUE SYSTEMS OF THE PEER CULTURE.

GROUP COHESIVENESS. By putting themselves into another's shoes, students can learn to accept individual differences and develop a sense of community within the group.

LEARNING SOCIAL BEHAVIOR WITH THE SUPPORT OF A COHESIVE GROUP. If the teacher has helped groups to develop a supportive climate, the students can explore various behaviors in different situations. This group climate can facilitate new learning.

LEARNING PROBLEM-SOLVING BEHAVIOR. By working through a problematic role-playing situation, the individual can learn problem-solving skills, since he has the opportunity to consider the consequences of his actions in a simulated environment. This can encourage the student to consider a variety of consequences before he acts in a particular way in future real-life situations.

Classroom Application

The Shaftels define nine steps in the teaching process of role playing:

1. "Warming up" the group (problem confrontation)
2. Selecting the participants (role players)
3. Setting the stage
4. Preparing the audience to participate as observers
5. Role playing (enactment)
6. Discussing and evaluating
7. Further enactments (replaying revised roles, playing suggested next steps or exploring alternative possibilities)
8. Further discussion
9. Sharing experiences and generalizing.[29]

"WARMING UP" THE GROUP. The purpose of this first step is to acquaint the class with the problem situation and stimulate their interest and involvement. This can be done with a specific example, sometimes through a "scene from a film, a television show incident," or any medium that conveys the problem in a stimulating manner.[30] The Shaftels also suggest that the problem story is very useful in initiating interest in a particular situation.

SELECTING PARTICIPANTS FOR ROLE PLAYING. Here the teacher tries to select students who identify with a role and who can feel the part. A student should not be forced into a role that is uncomfortable for him. However, the teacher may gradually work students into various roles. The shy student may not volunteer initially, and the teacher can ask this individual to take a less demanding role. The Shaftels suggest that for the first enactment the teacher choose students who will not immediately give an adult-oriented, socially acceptable solution, which may cut off conversation and exploration of various other solutions and consequences.

SETTING THE STAGE. Here the role players briefly outline their plan of attack. The students do not plan in detail what they will say or do; only general outlines are discussed. This is to ensure spontaneity during the actual enactment.

PREPARING THE AUDIENCE TO BE PARTICIPATING OBSERVERS. The teacher encourages the students to listen empathically to the role players and at the same time to consider alternative solutions to the enactment. The teacher can later inquire whether the role players acted in a realistic manner.

ROLE PLAYING. The teacher should encourage spontaneity in the role playing. Excesses in language and emotion should be avoided, but the students should feel that their actions are not subject to censure. The audience should also be made aware that the role a student plays does not reflect upon him as a person. Each role player is simply presenting the situation as he sees it. No one is evaluated for his acting; the emphasis is on exploring a situation.

DISCUSSION AND EVALUATION. This is an important part of the process. At first questions can focus on helping the class to think with the role players. Asking "How is Sally feeling?" or "What is Johnny thinking?" can help the class to relate their feelings and thoughts about the enactment. Later the discussion can center around alternative proposals.

As Mary says, "I don't think I'd do it that way," the teacher responds with "What would you do?" If no alternatives are offered, he may ask, "Is there some other way this situation might be resolved?"[31]

THE RE-ENACTMENT.   As alternative solutions arise, these can also be role-played. The same role players can re-enact the situation or other students can take part. Other students often are brought in when the first role player runs out of ideas. The new role player may learn that his alternative may not be as rational a solution as he originally imagined. Values for the individual slowly begin to become conscious as he moves from role playing to discussions and back to role playing.

SHARING EXPERIENCES AND GENERALIZING.   Here the students may volunteer personal experiences.

> Occasionally they offer personal experiences, but this should not be urged actively by the teacher since it may invite a child to expose himself to the group in ways that will harm his reputation. Therefore the teacher avoids asking, 'Did anything like this ever happen to you?' unless it is in an area that is not likely to rebound on individual children.[32]

The students can also generalize about a situation. Conclusions do not always come forth, but those that do arise are based on significant experiential learning. The Shaftels conclude: "We cannot command generalization; it is a product of individual insights based on much meaningful experience."[33]

These nine steps are summarized in the following example:[34]

ACTION	INTERPRETATION
TEACHER: "Do you remember the other day we had a discussion about Janey's lunch money? Because she had put her money in her pocket and had not given it to me when she came into the room, it was lost. We had quite a talk about finding money: whether to keep it or turn it in.	("Warming up" the group: Introducing the problem.) Utilizing an actual school incident to open up a problem area, sensitizing pupils to the problems.
"Sometimes it's not easy to decide what to do. Do you ever have times when you just don't know what to do?"	Creating a permissive environment: recognizing that it is not always easy to find a socially acceptable solution to a dilemma.
(There are nods in the group.)	

"I would like to read you a story this afternoon about a boy who found himself in just such a spot. His parents wanted him to do one thing, but his gang insisted he do something else. Trying to please everybody, he got himself into difficulty. This will be one of those problem stories which stop, but are not finished."

A PUPIL: "Like the one we did last week?"

TEACHER: "Yes."

A PUPIL: "Oh! But can't you give us one with an ending?"

TEACHER: "When you get into a jam, does someone always come along and tell you how your problem will end?"

PUPILS: "Oh, no! Not very often."

TEACHER: "In life, we usually have to make our own endings—we have to solve our problems ourselves. That's why I'm reading you these problem stories—so that we can practice endings—try out many different ones to see which work the best for us.

"As I read this story, you might be thinking of what you would do if you were in Tommy Haines' place."

(Teacher reads the story, "Clubhouse Boat," here summarized.)

Tommy Haines belongs to a club which the boys have organized in the neighborhood, the Mountain Lions. An uncle of one of the boys agrees to give them a houseboat for a club if they will have it repaired and docked in the town's yacht harbor.

Children indicate how meaningful the problem is for them by bodily and facial responses. Preparing the class to identify with the main character.

This class had already experienced several problem sessions.

This response is quite typical. Children are used to the "happy ending" pattern. The satisfaction that comes with increased ability to tackle and solve problems develops slowly, and only through opportunity to face problems.

Preparing the class to listen purposefully. This is a very important part of the process.

(The story constitutes an extended warmup or preparation for role playing.) Characters and actions are delineated and the problem situation is developed to its critical point.

Tommy agrees to pay his share of the repair bill, twenty dollars. He is confident that he can manage this, because he is earning money as delivery boy for a drugstore.

To his dismay, his father refuses to let him participate, insisting that he must put his earnings in the bank.

This places Tommy in difficulty with his gang. They have had the boat repaired and owe money for it. Pete "borrows" the money for Tommy out of a purse which had been left in his dad's taxicab by a patron.

Tommy, frantic to get together the amount he owes his gang, resorts to small subterfuges, deliberately working to talk people into giving him tips, not telling his folks that he has earned tips or that he has been given a raise in pay, and even keeping several small sums given him in overpayment on orders.

Finally, the boys are in difficulty. The woman returns for her purse, and Pete's parents learn that he took money from it. They threaten to go to all the boys' fathers unless the money is returned by the next morning.

The boys manage to chip in some more money, but cannot raise enough. They insist that Tommy find the balance needed.

Tommy worries. Then, after delivering a package for the druggist, Tommy discovers that the customer had made a mistake and overpaid him five dollars. Enough to clear the debt to the gang!

Tommy is deeply tempted. He stands in front of the customer's closed door. Shall he knock and return the money—or shall he leave and keep the money he needs so badly?

TEACHER: "What do you think Tommy will do?"

Stimulating the class to explore possible solutions. A spontaneous expression which probably reveals an impulse.

A PUPIL: "I think he'll keep the money! "

TEACHER: "Yes?—"

A PUPIL: "Because he needs to pay the club."

Analyzing the problem.

A PUPIL: "Oh, no, he won't. He'll get found out, and he knows it."

Anticipating consequences.

A PUPIL: "How can he? Nobody knows he has it."

Expressing a personal philosophy.

TEACHER: (to this last student) "Would you like to come up here, Jerry, and be Tommy? "

(Selecting participants.)

The teacher deliberately chooses the boy who expresses an antisocial solution.

(Jerry comes to the front of the room.)

"Jerry, whom will you need to help you?"

JERRY: "I'll need somebody to be the customer. And I'll need boys to be the gang."

Encouraging the pupil to describe his solution and situation himself.

(Players are chosen.)

The teacher invites several children to participate. The setting is arranged. One corner of the classroom is the school where the gang is waiting for Tommy to come with the needed money. A chair is placed in another corner to represent the door of the house to which the package is delivered.

While children are never urged to play roles which they do not "feel," occasionally a child needs to be encouraged to participate.

(Setting the stage.)

TEACHER: "Where are you going to start, Jerry?"

JERRY: "I'll deliver the package."

The teacher helps describe the furnishings needed and helps arrange them quickly.

TEACHER: "Very well. Now, you people, as you watch, consider

(Preparing the class to be participating observers.)

whether you think Jerry's way of ending the story could really happen. How will people feel? You may want to think of what will happen next. Perhaps you'll have different ideas about it; and when Jerry's finished, and we've talked about it, we can try your ideas."

FIRST ENACTMENT

(Tommy knocks on door. The boy playing role of old man "opens" the door.)

(Role playing.)
Pretend level.
A chair is used to designate the door.

TOMMY: "Delivery from Central Drugstore, sir. Eleven dollars and twenty-eight cents due."

MAN: "Here you are. And here's a quarter. Buy yourself a Cadillac."

(Man closes door. Tommy counts money. Discovers he has been overpaid five dollars. Raises hand to knock on door and call man back—then turns away. Walks across the classroom to the waiting gang.)

This boy chooses to "get away with it." His enactment is an expression of the (ethical) value and the antisocial behavior that have been causing concern among the school faculty.

TOMMY: "Hey, guys, look! I got the money we need. Here! "

EDDY: "Swell! Now we can pay for the boat. Come on, gang! "

(End of enactment.)

TEACHER: "Well, Jerry has given us one solution. What do you think of it? "

A PUPIL: "Uh-uh! It won't work!"

JERRY: "Why not?"

A PUPIL: "That man is going to remember how much money he had. He'll phone the druggist about it."

JERRY: "So what? He can't prove

(Discussing and evaluating.) Encouraging an evaluation. The teacher is careful to be noncommittal.
A judgment.

It happens that Jerry is a boy of low mental ability; he is quite sure of himself.

An analysis of consequences.

anything on me. I'll just say he didn't overpay me."

A PUPIL: "You'll lose your job."

JERRY: "When they can't prove it?"

ANOTHER PUPIL: "Yes. Even if they can't prove it! "

TEACHER: "Why do you think so, John? "

JOHN: "Because the druggist has to be on the side of his customer. He can fire Tommy and hire another boy. But he doesn't want his customers mad at him."

A PUPIL: "He's going to feel pretty sick inside if he keeps the money."

Other consequences are here foreseen—anxiety and guilt.

TEACHER: "What do you mean? "

Encouraging further expression.

PUPIL: "Well, it bothers you when you know you've done something wrong."

TEACHER: "Do you have any other way to solve this problem? "

(Exploring for other solutions.)

PUPIL: "Yes. Tommy should knock on the door and tell the customer about being overpaid. Maybe the man'll let Tommy keep the money."

A proposal with a wishful (fantasy) solution.

TEACHER: "All right, let's try it your way, Dick."

The teacher follows through. The consequences of fantasy solutions should be explored.

SECOND ENACTMENT

(New role players are selected, and the scene is set. Tommy delivers the parcel, is paid; the door is shut. He discovers that he has been overpaid five dollars.)

TOMMY: "Gosh, I better knock and call that man back! "

(He knocks.)

MAN (opening door): "What is it, son? "

TOMMY: "Sir, you overpaid me five dollars."

MAN: "I did! Well—you're an honest boy. Tell you what—you keep the change."

(End of enactment.)

TEACHER: "What about this solution?"

SEVERAL PUPILS: "It's all right! It's fine. That settles everything."

TEACHER: "Do you think this could really happen?"

A PUPIL: "Yes. Because once I got overpaid for my paper delivery, and when I told the man, he said, "Keep it.""

TEACHER: "How much money did he overpay you?"

A PUPIL: "A dollar and a quarter."

TEACHER: "Do you think it might be different with five dollars?"

PUPIL: "Yes. That's too much. He might give you a dollar tip."

TEACHER: "How do the rest of you feel about this?"

(The class agrees that few adults would tip five dollars.)

"Then how shall Tommy solve his problem?"

A PUPIL: "I think he should talk it over with his mother."

TEACHER: "Why his mother, Alice?"

ALICE: "Well, when my dad says no, I ask my mother."

(Grins and nods from the group.)

TEACHER: "Is that the way it works for you all?"

A PUPIL: "No, it's the other way around in our house."

(Further discussion.)

The teacher remains noncommittal. The class accepts a fantasy solution.

The teacher pushes for a realistic evaluation. Generalizing from personal experience.

Exploring the analogy for parallels.

Again pushing for reality.

A more realistic evaluation.

Involving the rest of the class.

Guiding the class to see that they have not yet found a realistic solution to the story. This is probably the pupil's pattern of dealing with troubling dilemmas.

The mechanisms that work for some.

Again exploring with the class.

ANOTHER PUPIL: "My folks stick together. Kids just don't have a chance."	Different families have different relationships.
TEACHER: "You feel that grown-ups just don't understand? "	Reflecting a child's thoughts so that he may explore further.
A PUPIL: "Well, sometimes they jump to conclusions."	
TEACHER: "Do you feel that Tommy's parents were wrong? "	Guiding the thinking.
A PUPIL: "No. Tommy had no business promising so much money without asking his parents."	A judgment made.
A PUPIL: "That was too much money for kids to spend."	
A PUPIL: "But once he promised it his dad should have helped him out."	A concept of the father role.
A PUPIL: "My mother would help me out of a jam! "	A mother-child relationship expressed.
TEACHER: "Would you like to play this, Sally, the way you think it could happen with your mother? "	The teacher seizes the opportunity to explore a constructive solution, now that the class has already explored an antisocial solution and a fantasy solution.

THIRD ENACTMENT

(The setting is Tommy's home.)	(Another enactment.)
TOMMY: "Mom, I'm in an awful jam! "	
MOTHER: "What's the trouble, Tommy? "	
(Tommy tells his mother the whole story.)	
MOTHER: "Why, Tommy, you should have told me sooner. Here, you pay the money (opens purse) and we'll talk this over with your dad when he comes home."	Mother will help, but children do get punished, in this version.
(End of enactment.)	
TEACHER: "What will happen now? "	Probing for consequences.
A PUPIL: "Tommy will get a licking! "	

TEACHER: "How do you feel about that?"

A PUPIL: "It's all right. I'd rather have the licking and get it off my mind."

TEACHER: "Does this sound familiar, class? Do you know of an instance in which a boy or girl had to make such a decision?"

JIM: "Yes, it happened to me once. I was borrowing money from all the milk bottles on our street. It got so I couldn't sleep nights worrying about it. Finally, my Pop caught up with me and gave me an awful licking. And was I glad."

TEACHER: "You mean, it was a relief not to have to worry about getting caught?"

JIM: "Yes."

TEACHER: "Sometimes we get into things we wish we'd never started. Was that Tommy's trouble?"

PUPILS: "Yes."

A PUPIL: "But he should have told his dad. He'd have helped him out."

TEACHER: "Why was his father so strict?"

PUPIL: "Because he wanted to teach Tommy a lesson from his own experience."

TEACHER: "Do you think that a father should help his boy decide what to do with the money he earns?"

Reaching a definite attitude on the problem.

(Sharing experiences.)

Tying the situation in with known experience in a nonthreatening way. If a child wishes, he may describe someone else's experience rather than admit his own mistakes.

This child chose to be direct and frank.

The teacher is careful to be noncritical and casual and to generalize. Any sort of discussion in a permissive atmosphere may elicit such admissions of individual behavior. The teacher should safeguard a pupil from any teasing or loss of respect from his peers.

Exploring the attitude of fathers.

Opening up a new phase of the problem.

The Teacher's Role

The teacher should establish a climate of trust in which the students feel it is relatively "safe" to experiment with behaviors. Thus, the teacher is nonjudgmental and supportive. The teacher can accept "negative" feelings in order to explore the various consequences of such feelings. The teacher should also be a good listener as he creates a climate in which the class is attentive to enactment and discussion.

The teacher is not nondirective, however. He intervenes along the nine steps of the process to facilitate insight and understanding. He does not let the process collapse at any one point but keeps it moving. However, the teacher lets the student make his own decisions during this process.

Applicability of the Model

This model has wide applicability since it can be used at all educational levels. It is limited only by the resources and imagination of the teacher. Some students, however, resist role playing because they don't want to express their feelings. As a result only a few students in a particular class may do most of the role playing. As mentioned earlier, some students should gradually be worked into various roles.

The Learning Environment

The role-playing model is nurturant, since conditions are created which assist in the development of self-concept, problem-solving skills, and group cohesiveness.

Figure 8

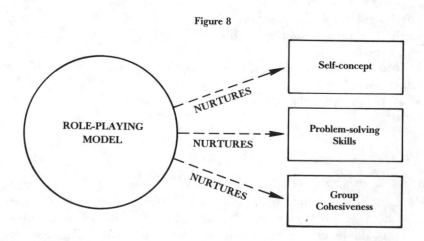

SELF-DIRECTED MODEL

Carl Rogers, a psychologist, is one of the fathers of the human-potential movement and affective education. His "Personal Thoughts on Teaching and Learning" remains a classic statement on affective education. Some of these statements can also be seen as a rationale for self-directed learning.

> It seems to me that anything that can be taught to another is relatively inconsequential, and has little or no significant influence on behavior. . . .
>
> I realize increasingly that I am only interested in learning which significantly influences behavior. . . .
>
> I have come to feel that the only learning which significantly influences behavior is self-discovered, self-appropriated learning.
>
> Such self-discovered learning, truth that has been personally appropriated and assimilated in experience, cannot be directly communicated to another. . . .
>
> As a consequence of the above, I realize that I have lost interest in being a teacher.
>
> I realize that I am only interested in being a learner, preferably learning things that matter, that have some significant influence on my own behavior.[35]

Rogers is saying that the student is the only person who can define the goals for learning and take responsibility for that learning. The learning group or the class becomes a mechanism for supporting individual development. The goal of self-directed learning is fully functioning people

> who are able to take self-initiated action to be responsible for those actions;
> who are capable of intelligent choice and self-direction;
> who are critical learners, able to evaluate the contributions made by others;
> who have acquired knowledge relevant to the solution of problems;
> who, even more importantly, are able to adapt flexibly and intelligently to new problem situations;
> who have internalized an adaptive mode of approach to problems, utilizing all pertinent experience freely and creatively;
> who are able to cooperate effectively with others in these various activities;

who work, not for the approval of others, but in terms of their own socialized purposes.[36]

The fully functioning person also is in touch with his feelings and inner being in an immediate and open way.

> Such a person experiences in the present with immediacy. He is able to live in his feelings and reactions of the moment. He is not bound by the structure of his past learnings but these are a present resource for him insofar as they relate to the experience of the moment. He lives freely, subjectively, in an existential confrontation with this moment of life. . . .It seems to me that the clients who have moved most significantly in therapy live more intimately with their feelings of pain, but also more vividly with their feelings of ecstasy; that anger is more clearly felt, but so also is life; that fear is an experience they know more deeply, but so is courage; and the reason they can thus live more fully in a wider range is that they have this underlying confidence in themselves as trustworthy instruments for encountering life. . . .[37]

Classroom Application

Self-directed learning involves two basic steps. The first is for the teacher or facilitator to create a climate of trust and openness in which self-direction can occur. The second step is for the individual or the group to work out a self-directed plan for learning and development. The sixth-grade teacher's class cited in Chapter 2 is an example of this process. The teacher set a climate for experimentation and then allowed one group to negotiate its own learning contracts.

Another example is found in *On Becoming a Person,* in which Dr. S. Tenenbaum describes a college course taught by Rogers on "The Process of Personality Change." Twenty-five students attended the course, and Tenenbaum's description is an example of self-directed learning in a group context.

On the first day of class Rogers said it would be nice if the students introduced themselves and stated their purposes. A strained silence followed. Gradually students introduced themselves.

Rogers informed the class that he had articles and other printed materials which might be useful to them, but he did not make any "assignments." He also told the class that he had some tapes and films of therapy sessions to which they could listen if they wished. This initial session was followed by four rather frustrating classes. Students spoke randomly, and there was little direction. Rogers, however, listened to every statement with attention and regard and thus created a climate for self-direction. Some of the students eventually became angry and told Rogers that they wanted more direction. Since they felt that he was the authority, they demanded that he lecture to them. Tenenbaum says the class was becoming an intense and lively experience.

> Queerly enough, from the outset, even in their anger, the members of the group felt joined together, and outside the classroom, there was an excitement and a ferment, for even in their frustration, they had communicated as never before in any classroom, and probably never before in quite the way they had. The class was bound together by a common, unique experience. In the Rogers class, they had spoken their minds; the words did not come from a book, nor were they the reflection of the instructor's thinking, nor that of any other authority. The ideas, emotions and feelings came from themselves; and this was the releasing and the exciting process.[38]

The students kept pressing Rogers to be more directive. At one point he responded to a suggestion that he lecture for an hour. He then read an unpublished paper he had written. The class felt a letdown during and after the lecture since the emotional tone was so different from that of the previous sessions. After this experience, according to Tenenbaum, the group became an interacting organism. "The instructor also joined in, but his role, more important than any in the group, somehow became merged with the group: the group was important, the center, the base of operation, not the instructor."[39]

The sessions then became very meaningful for the participants. For example,

> As they interacted, there were moments of insight and revelation and understanding that were almost awesome in nature; they were what, I believe, Rogers would describe as "moments of therapy," those pregnant moments when you see a human soul revealed before you, in all its breathless wonder; and then a silence, almost like reverence, would overtake the class. And each member of the class became enveloped with a warmth and a loveliness that border on the mystic. I for one, and I am quite

sure the others also, never had an experience quite like this. It was learning and therapy; and by therapy I do not mean [treatment of] illness, but what might be characterized by a healthy change in the person, an increase in his flexibility, his openness, his willingness to listen. In the process, we all felt elevated, freer, more accepting of ourselves and others, more open to new ideas, trying hard to understand and accept.[40]

There was still some hostility, but individuals were more accepting of each other's differences. There were also moments when someone dominated the group, but eventually the group would "right" itself, not "by setting rules but by its own being." In other words, the individuals established a climate or atmosphere that prevented the group from becoming dysfunctional.

Dr. Tenenbaum felt that the group produced some important changes in behavior.

In the course of this process, I saw hard, inflexible, dogmatic persons, in the brief period of several weeks, change in front of my eyes and become sympathetic, understanding and to a marked degree non-judgmental. I saw neurotic, compulsive persons ease up and become more accepting of themselves and others. In one instance, a student who particularly impressed me by his change, told me when I mentioned this: "It is true. I feel less rigid, more open to the world. And I like myself better for it. I don't believe I ever learned so much anywhere." I saw shy persons become less shy and aggressive persons more sensitive and moderate.[41]

Thus Tenenbaum's perceptions indicated that many of the group members moved toward Rogers' goal of a fully functioning person. It should be noted, however, that formal research has not supported some of the profound changes reported by members of the self-directed group.

Tenenbaum also reports that some of the group continued to be displeased with the nondirective method. Three or four students found the experience distasteful and uncomfortable, and wanted more structure and formal content.

Rogers allowed the students to grade themselves. He never summarized during the course or sought closure on any issue. He saw the class and personal development as an ongoing process with no end.

The Teacher's Role

It is important, of course, that the teacher not control or domi-nate the group but let things unfold. However, he does help set the overall climate.

Carl Rogers in particular has mentioned qualities in teachers that are generally facilitative of healthy human relations, nota-bly realness, regard, and empathy. Realness is the capacity to be in tune with or congruent with one's own feelings and concerns. It means not putting on a facade but accepting feelings and dealing with them at a conscious level. An example of this is the behavior of a teacher who made art materials available to her students for creative work but was bothered by the chaos of the room:

> **I find it maddening to live with the mess—with a capital M! No one seems to care except me. Finally, one day, I told the children . . . that I am a neat, orderly person by nature and that the mess was driving me to distraction. Did they have a solution? It was suggested there were some volunteers who could clean up. . . . I said it didn't seem fair to me to have the same people clean up all the time for others—but it would solve it for me. "Well, some people like to clean up," they replied. So that's the way it is.[42]**

Regard concerns the teacher's ability to convey respect for the individual student and his potential for growth. It also involves the teacher's respect for the student's right to make decisions affecting his growth. Regard does not involve relinquishing au-thority but means that the teacher conveys his sense of respect of the student's concerns, feelings, and values.

Empathy involves the teacher's ability to understand the student's perceptions and to convey that understanding. It means trying to put oneself in the student's shoes. The work of Piaget and Erikson indicates that children view the world much differ-ently than adults do. If the teacher is not aware of the child's perspective, the child's growth may be thwarted.

Research studies have supported the notion that teacher real-ness, regard, and empathy are positively related to student devel-opment. This seems to hold true for emotional development as well as development in such areas as reading achievement. In sum, certain skills and capacities are required to be an effective facilitator of the self-directed group. If the leader is inadequate the group experience can be unpleasant or even harmful.

The responsibility for learning lies with the learner, but the teacher must gather adequate resources so that the individual student can pursue the line of inquiry that interests him.

Applicability of the Model

This model is relevant to a number of settings; however, the students and teacher must be able to deal with ambiguity. It is not applicable to lower stage CL students. The general climate of the school should be supportive, since self-directed learning is usually not limited to the classroom but extends to other parts of the school (e.g., use of the library) and to the community as well.

The Learning Environment

The self-directed model is nurturant, since it creates conditions that are conducive to development of the fully functioning person.

Figure 9

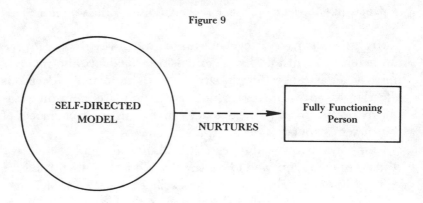

SUMMARY: SELF-CONCEPT MODELS

	Values Clarification	Identity Education	Classroom Meeting Model	Role-Playing Model	Self-Directed Model
Aims	To clarify personal values. To respect the values of others	To gain a positive self-image, a relatedness to others, and self-control	To develop a sense of identity through responsible decision making	To develop positive self-concept, problem-solving skills, and group cohesiveness	To become a fully functioning person
Teaching Process	1. choosing freely 2. choosing from alternatives 3. choosing after consideration of consequences 4. prizing and cherishing 5. publicly affirming, when appropriate 6. acting 7. acting with a pattern, consistency and repetition	1. determine learner characteristics 2. ascertain learner concerns 3. diagnose concerns 4. determine outcomes 5. outline organizing ideas 6. choose content vehicles 7. choose learning skills 8. finalize teaching procedures 9. evaluate	1. teacher creates climate of involvement 2. teacher or student raises problem for discussion 3. student makes personal value judgement 4. teacher and student identify different courses of action 5. student commits himself to one course of action 6. teacher and students follow up student commitment	1. warming up the group 2. selecting participants 3. preparing the audience to participate as observers 4. setting the stage 5. role playing 6. discussing and evaluating 7. further enactments 8. further discussion 9. sharing experiences and generalizing	Teacher creates an open climate, then the individual sets his own learning pattern
Teacher's Role	Teacher should be warm and accepting and create an atmosphere for sharing values	Teacher should be tuned into student concerns and relate curriculum to those concerns	Teacher should create a climate of involvement and also press student for commitment	Teacher provides open climate for role experimentation and keeps the role-playing sequence moving	Facilitator should be empathic and genuine and convey respect for students. He should also make resources available to students
Amount of Structure	High	Moderate	Moderate	Moderate	Low

Notes

1. Quoted in Erik Erikson, *Identity: Youth and Crisis* (New York: Norton, 1968), p. 19.
2. Sidney Simon, Leland Howe, and Howard Kirschenbaum, *Values Clarification: A Handbook of Practical Strategies* (New York: Hart, 1972), p. 15.
3. Louis Raths, Merrill Harmin, and Sidney Simon, *Values and Teaching: Working with Values in the Classroom* (Columbus, Ohio: Charles Merrill, 1966), pp. 28–29.
4. Simon, Howe, and Kirschenbaum, *Values Clarification*, p. 33.
5. Ibid., p. 34.
6. Ibid., p. 199.
7. Ibid., p. 201.
8. Ibid., p. 75.
9. Howard Kirschenbaum, "Beyond Values Clarification," in *Readings in Values Clarification*, edited by H. Kirschenbaum, and Sidney B. Simon (Minneapolis, Minn.: Winston Press, 1973), pp. 92–110.
10. Gerald Weinstein and Mario Fantini, *Toward Humanistic Education: A Curriculum of Affect* (New York: Praeger, 1970), p. 34.
11. Ibid., p. 35.
12. Ibid., p. 42.
13. Ibid., pp. 123–25.
14. Ibid., pp. 49–50.
15. Ibid., p. 58.
16. Ibid., pp. 68–71.
17. William Glasser, *Schools Without Failure* (New York: Harper & Row, 1969), pp. 13–14.
18. Ibid., p. 13.
19. Ibid., p. 21.
20. Ibid., pp. 21–22.
21. Ibid., p. 126.
22. Ibid., p. 134.
23. Ibid., p. 178.
24. Ibid., pp. 140–41.
25. Ibid., pp. 155–61.
26. Fannie and George Shaftel, *Role Playing for Social Values: Decision-Making in the Social Studies* (Englewood Cliffs, N.J.: Prentice-Hall, 1967), p. 8.
27. Ibid., p. 35.
28. Ibid., pp. 38–39.
29. Ibid., pp. 65–66.
30. Ibid., p. 75.
31. Ibid., p. 80.
32. Ibid., p. 82.
33. Ibid., p. 83.
34. Ibid., pp. 67–74. (Reprinted with permission.)
35. Carl Rogers, *On Becoming a Person* (Boston: Houghton Mifflin, 1961), p. 276.
36. Carl Rogers, *Client-Centered Therapy* (Boston: Houghton Mifflin, 1951), pp. 387–88.
37. Carl Rogers, "Toward Becoming a Fully Functioning Person," *Perceiving, Behaving, Becoming,* Association for Supervision and Curriculum Development Yearbook (Washington, D.C.: National Education Association, 1962), p. 31.
38. Rogers, *On Becoming a Person*, pp. 301–2.

39. Ibid., p. 304.
40. Ibid., p. 305.
41. Ibid., p. 306.
42. Carl Rogers., *Freedom to Learn* (Columbus, Ohio: Charles Merrill, 1969), p. 108.

OTHER MODELS AND BIBLIOGRAPHY

Other Models

Achievement Motivation
Developed by David McClelland and Alfred Alschuler, achievement motivation instructs the student to set realistic expectations and develop motivation to meet these expectations. This model includes exercises in such other areas as communications, self-awareness, and values clarification. An explanation of the approach can be found in *Teaching Achievement Motivation* by Alfred Alschuler, Diane Tabor, and James McIntyre (Middletown, Conn.: Education Ventures, 1971).

Process Education
Terry Borton has created a model based on student concerns, similar to identity education. The teacher indentifies student concerns and then develops activities to facilitate a positive self-identity. Process education is explained in Borton's *Reach, Touch and Teach* (New York: McGraw Hill, 1970).

Simulation
Simulation provides another framework for role playing; often the two terms are used interchangeably. Texts that can be used as introductions to simulation are S. Boocock and E.O. Scheld (eds.), *Simulation Games in Learning* (Beverly Hills, California: Sage, 1968) and John Taylor and Rex Walford, *Simulation in the Classroom* (Baltimore, Md.: Penguin Books, 1972).

Bibliography

Glasser, W. *Reality Therapy.* New York: Harper & Row, 1965. Glasser describes in detail the theory and practice of reality therapy, which is the rationale behind the social-problem-solving meeting.

――――. *Schools Without Failure.* New York: Harper & Row, 1969. Glasser applies his reality therapy to the classroom and presents a number of practical suggestions for using the classroom meeting.

Hawley, Robert C. *Human Values in the Classroom.* Amherst, Mass.: Education Research Associates, 1973. Discusses a model of values clarification similar to Simon's and a number of other issues including grades, discipline, and using classroom space.

Howe, Leland, and Howe, Mary M. *Personalizing Education: Values Clarification and Beyond.* New York: Hart, 1975. A large book filled with activities in values clarification, communications, goal setting, and classroom management procedures.

Raths, Louis E.; Harmin, Merrill; and Simon, Sidney B. *Values and Teaching: Working with Values in the Classroom.* Columbus, Ohio: Charles Merrill, 1966. The original work on values clarification. It describes the theoretical origins of the approach along with a number of classroom activities.

Rogers, Carl. *Freedom to Learn.* Columbus, Ohio: Charles Merrill, 1969. One of the seminal texts in affective education. Rogers presents examples of experiential learning with an emphasis on the intensive group experience.

Shaftel, Fannie R. *Value in Action: Role-Playing Problems for the Intermediate Grades.* New York: Holt, Rinehart & Winston, 1969. Filmstrips are included in these materials, which present open-ended problems for role playing. The materials are based on Shaftel and Shaftel, *Role Playing for Social Values.*

Shaftel, Fannie R., and Shaftel, George. *Role Playing for Social Values: Decision Making in the Social Studies.* Englewood Cliffs, N.J.: Prentice-Hall, 1967. Contains the rationale for role playing as well as practical suggestions for developing enactment situations. A number of open-ended stories are included to initiate role playing.

Simon, Sidney; Howe, Leland; and Kirschenbaum, Howard. *Values Clarification: A Handbook of Practical Strategies.* New York: Hart, 1972. The focus here is on classroom activities. There are approximately 80 strategies for the teacher to choose from.

Weinstein, Gerald, and Fantini, Mario D., (eds.). *Toward Humanistic Education: A Curriculum of Affect.* New York: Praeger, 1970. Presents a model of curriculum development based on student concerns as well as several practical examples of identity education.

CHAPTER 5
SENSITIVITY AND GROUP ORIENTATION

The teaching models discussed in this chapter focus on openness and sensitivity to others. However, most of these models assume that openness occurs within a framework of conscious identity. Often there is a correlation between sensitivity to others and a consciously developed self-concept. An example of this relationship is described by Rogers:

> **I find such a person to be sensitively open to all of his experience—sensitive to what is going on in his environment, sensitive to other individuals with whom he is in relationship, and sensitive perhaps most of all to the feelings, reactions and emergent meanings which he discovers in himself. The fear of some aspects of his own experience continues to diminish, so that more and more of his life is available to him.[1]**

Four models of teaching to facilitate openness and sensitivity are presented. The *communications model,* developed by the psychologist Robert Carkhuff, develops specific communication skills or conditions (empathy, genuineness, etc.) that are integral to effective interpersonal functioning. Carkhuff has done a great deal of research to support the effectiveness of his approach and its relationship to human development.

English educator Peter McPhail's model facilitates sensitivity to and consideration of another person's needs and feelings. The *sensitivity-consideration model* and the curriculum materials associated with it often place the student in another person's shoes. Through empathy, the student gains understanding of other people and incorporates this understanding in moral decision making.

Transactional analysis as a model of teaching can be used to analyze classroom interaction. It is useful in eliminating "games" played by teachers and students and in facilitating open communications. Transactional analysis also can help teacher and students to change dysfunctional behavior patterns.

Human relations training provides an environment in which the student can learn to function effectively in a group as well as to develop sensitivity to others' behavior. Although human relations training in its pure form cannot be applied to the classroom, many of the exercises and principles associated with the model can be used by the teacher.

The teaching models in this chapter range in structure from high to low. The communications model is high in structure, the sensitivity-consideration model is moderate in structure, and transactional analysis and human relations training are moderate to low in structure.

COMMUNICATIONS MODEL

Robert Carkhuff and his associates have developed a training model that focuses on specific communication conditions which they argue are necessary for effective interpersonal functioning. These conditions include empathy, genuineness, respect, specificity of expression, self-disclosure, confrontation, and immediacy. Carkhuff also states that these conditions can be measured, and he has developed rating scales for this purpose—for example, a 1-to-5 scale for rating empathy.[2] At the lowest level, "the . . . person appears completely unaware or ignorant of even the most conspicuous surface feelings of the other person"; at the highest level, the person "almost always responds with accurate empathic understanding to all of the other person's deeper feelings as well as surface feelings." Respect or positive regard is also rated on a 1-to-5 scale. At level 1, the person is "communicating clear negative regard" for the other. At level 5, the person "communicates a very deep respect" for the other. At level 1 on the genuineness scale, "the . . . person's verbalizations are clearly unrelated to what he is feeling at the moment, or his only genuine responses are negative to what he is feeling as regards the second person." At level 5, the person "is freely and deeply himself in a nonexploitative relationship" with the other person. Relevant concreteness or specificity of expression is also defined, again by a 5-point scale. At the lowest level, "the first person leads or allows all discussion with the second person to deal only with vague and anonymous generalities." At the highest level, the person "is always helpful in guiding discussion so that the second person may discuss fluently, directly and completely specific feelings and experiences."

Using the scales, Carkhuff has conducted research that has demonstrated a relationship between these conditions and human development. For example, teachers who rank high on empathy, respect, and genuineness are more likely to facilitate cognitive and affective growth in their students than teachers who rank low.[3] Other studies have indicated that these communication conditions are integral to effective interpersonal functioning. In sum, the Carkhuff method attempts to develop communication skills that are important to human interaction and development.

Classroom Application

The Carkhuff method is a highly structured communication model. It can be conducted with several small groups in the classroom, or individual students can work through the training while the rest of the class acts as observers. The process involves one student who acts as a helper and another who is the "helpee." The helpee either verbalizes something of real concern to himself or role-plays a problem situation. The helper in responding to him attempts to communicate effectively, using one or more of the scales to guide his responses. For example, he might use the empathy scale to "respond with accuracy to all the person's deeper as well as surface feelings." After the helper has completed his response, the other group members rate it, using the empathy scale as a guide. The scales form the basis for the two main elements in the Carkhuff programs: communications training (the helper's response) and discrimination training (the observers' ratings of his response).

An excerpt from a Carkhuff session might clarify the procedures. For example:

TRAINEE 1 (acting as helpee):   Uh, it's an empty life. It's, um, there is, uh, no depth to it at all. I mean you just talk about very, very superficial things, and the first few times, it's O.K. But then after that, there's nothing to talk about. So you drink and you pretend to be happy over silly jokes and silly things that people do when they all, uh, are trying to impress one another, and they're very materialistic, and uh, it's just not the route I want to go.

TRAINEE 2 (acting as helper):   So your feelings are so strong that you just can't fake it any more.

TRAINER: O.K. How would you rate the helper's response on the empathy scale?

TRAINEE 3:   I'd give him a 3.

TRAINEE 4:   3.5.

TRAINEE 5:   3.

TRAINEE 6:   4.

TRAINEE 7:   3.5.

TRAINEE 8:   3.5.[4]

The trainer then gives his rating and his rationale for the rating.

This same pattern is repeated with other students acting as helper or helpee and using other rating scales to shape and discriminate responses. The teacher might also participate as a helper to offer a model for effective interpersonal functioning.

In the following situation, parents are the trainees. One parent, Joe, role-plays his son, while another parent, Ann, role-plays the helper.

JOE: So, I wasn't going to fire them off. I was just trying to sell them.

ANN: So you feel that it was perfectly all right to have these firecrackers?

JOE: Well, why not? Everybody else had them. I'm not the only one, and I wasn't going to shoot them off. I just wanted to make a little money.

ANN: And you feel that the principal treated you as though you had broken the law?

JOE: Well, yeah! I mean, they all jumped on me, and after all I didn't shoot anything off, so Dopey over there shot one off and tipped the whole thing. If he hadn't done it nobody would have found out.

ANN: And then it wouldn't have been wrong for you to have taken them there in the first place?

JOE: Why, no. Of course not.

ANN: You think, then, that it was the fault of the boy who shot off one of these firecrackers?

JOE: Well, they were just little bitty ones—I mean, even if he did shoot one off, what's the damage with that? Nothing got broken, nothing got burned up.

ANN: And nobody got hurt.

JOE: No.

ANN: But they could have, huh?

JOE: Well, I don't know. But nothing went wrong except that I got blamed for it.

ANN: None of the other boys got blamed?

JOE: Oh, yeah—they caught the other guys with it but I got the worst of it. They jumped on me—she goes calling you up on the telephone.

ANN: Would you have told me about it if she hadn't called me?

JOE: Well, no.

ANN: Well, if you thought it was all right to do this, what would have been the harm, then, in telling me?

JOE: You know as well as I do that you would have taken them away from me.

ANN: And you don't think that you ever would have shot one of these things off—the ones that you didn't sell? Would you really have done this?

JOE: Well, I was going to sell them. I wouldn't have any to shoot off.

ANN: Well, what if you didn't sell them all? What would you have done with the rest of them?

JOE: Well, I don't know. I would have shot them.

ANN: Oh? But you know that's against the law.

JOE: Oh, so what?

ANN: And you feel that getting caught was the real crime?

JOE: Well, yeah!

ANN: But no harm was done unless you got caught?

JOE: Sure—well—that's—(I'm losing the phraseology and I should remember it)—but—yeah, as long as you don't get caught. What the heck.

ANN: So you feel that the principal and the teachers and the kids around you—they're the ones at fault, right?

JOE: Well, listen, there are always those finks—this one in particular. He's always, always getting me in trouble and the other guys in trouble, too. I'm not the only one. They blame it on me but there's Jack and Jim . . .

ANN: Why do you suppose they do that? Why do you suppose they single you out to put the blame on?

JOE: Oh, I don't know.

ANN: Do you suppose it could be because of other things that you've done?

JOE: Well, the other guys have been doing other stuff, too, all the time.

ANN: But they don't get caught?

JOE: No. They don't get the kind of stuff I do.

ANN: All right.

JOE: That's just about where it ended up anyway . . .

ANN: Uh huh. It did.

JOE: This being a packet of firecrackers he had picked up from another kid in the neighborhood and he took them down to school with him yesterday to peddle them off to the boys—to get a few cents.

TRAINER: All right. I'm going to follow a routine, but let's go quick around on the ratings. I want you to comment. I want you to dig in a little bit.

JOE: I'm trying to play it back—about as I remember, it's a 3.

KAREN: I'm just trying to think. She was—she was understanding in what he was saying and yet . . .

TRAINER: Somehow it didn't go anywhere.

KAREN: She was definitely the mother.

TRAINER: O.K. Give it a rating. Good. That's good.

KAREN: Oh, I would say she was—as far as understanding I would say she was about a 3.

TRAINER: Tony?

TONY: I say a solid 3.

TRAINER: All right. Let's go around once and then pick up . . .

STAN: Pushing 4—hard on a 4.

MARY: I agree that it was a 4.

IRENE: 3 to 4.

TOM: 3.

BILL: I said 3.5.

JANE: It's a 5.

TRAINER:　All right. Let's pick up where you left off.

KAREN:　Well, I was rating it in a way we rated it before. She was—she didn't seem to give him any . . .

TRAINER:　. . . direction. Now we come pretty fully around. It was helpful along the way—now we're coming pretty fully around to realizing the limitations of the kind of rating we've been doing.

KAREN:　Yeah.

TRAINER:　And yet we want to know that whatever she's going to do is going to be based in a good level of understanding. All right. Tony?

TONY:　Yeah, I felt that it was a good 3. I thought she was hearing what he was saying but I—(laugh)—couldn't help but share the same feeling. I didn't know where to go with it. I wouldn't have . . .

TRAINER:　That's where you were, Tony—you know—"O.K. So even if I dig in, 'What the hell do I do with this?' "

TONY:　I had the same thing happen. I didn't know where to go with it. I got this far and I couldn't . . .

JOE:　You see, that's the point. You're not fooling anyone. The agreement is there. You're reading . . .

TRAINER:　Right. Right.[5]

The teacher, then, employs the following steps in this teaching model. First, a student grouping pattern for the exercises is determined. Second, one student as helpee presents a problem. Third, the student helper attempts to respond to the helpee's concern, using the scales to guide his responses. Fourth, the other students and the teacher rate the helper responses and give their reasons for the ratings. These steps are then repeated with other students acting as helpee and helper.

The Teacher's Role

The teacher should keep the focus on communication skills and not solely on the issues raised by the student who is acting as helpee. It might be advisable to role-play situations in the beginning rather than discuss "real problems," in order to keep the focus on the communication skills. The teacher should also make sure that everyone has an opportunity to practice the various communication skills required. More emphasis should be placed on the communication aspect than on the discrimination phase lest the students become so "uptight" that learning the communication conditions is hindered.

The teacher should have some training in this method in order to work with the scales and to be an effective model for the communication skills. He should rate high in empathy, genuineness, and the other conditions that Carkhuff suggests are necessary for healthy human functioning.

This is a highly structured approach to communications training since the scales provide a framework for guiding and rating group interaction.

Applicability of the Model

This model would seem to be most relevant to the secondary-school and post-secondary-school settings. Because of its high structure, it offers a good starting point for developing communication skills, and this means it has potentially wide applicability. On the other hand, its applicability is limited if adequate pre-service or in-service training is not available to the teacher.

Figure 10

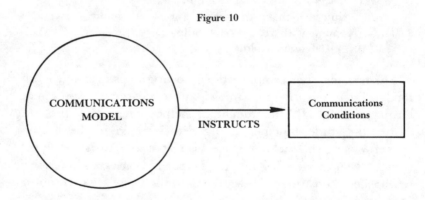

The Learning Environment

The learning environment is instructional as the student learns communication conditions through discrimination and communications training.

SENSITIVITY-CONSIDERATION MODEL

Peter McPhail, in association with the Schools Council Project in Moral Education in Britain, has developed a series of materials in moral education to nurture students' sensitivity to other individuals' needs and feelings. The first stage of the series is called *In Other People's Shoes*. Its main purpose is to develop "more consideration" of others' interests and feelings. An important aspect of the McPhail approach is that the materials were developed with the help of students, who identified the key situations for the materials.

In Other People's Shoes is divided into three units: Sensitivity, Consequences, and Points of View, which together comprise a model of teaching sensitivity and consideration. The focus of this model is to increase the secondary-school student's awareness of another individual's concerns and to help him incorporate this awareness into decision making that affects others.

> The only therapeutic hypothesis behind this material is that its use by a group working together may increase the individual group member's awareness of his own and other people's feelings, of how people are likely to behave in a number of situations, and of the value and reward of taking others' interests into account when acting. Ultimately we hope that such work will help boys and girls to take better courses of action because considerate solutions are rewarded in the group context. "Consideration" is discovered as a pleasant style of life.[6]

SENSITIVITY.   In the sensitivity unit, McPhail provides several work cards, each illustrating a situation designed to develop consideration. Some of these situations are listed below.

1.   You are very attracted to a girl/boy but she/he ignores you.
2.   A boy or girl of your own age, with whom you are friendly, appears to be very upset for some reason unknown to you.
3.   You suggest to a friend that you both go on the "big wheel" at a fair, but your friend seems reluctant.
4.   You know that your best friend is doing something which is causing him or her to suffer.
5.   A boy at school frequently "picks on" you, bullies you or insults you.[7]

McPhail suggests that there are a number of possible responses to each of these situations. He characterizes these possible responses as passive, passive-emotional, dependent-adult, dependent-peer, aggressive, very aggressive, avoidance, experimental-crude, experimental-sophisticated, mature-conventional, and mature-imaginative. McPhail has found that students tend to move from a "dependent-adult" stage at about age eleven to "experimental" behavior, which reaches a peak at around fourteen or fifteen. At about seventeen the students attain "mature" behavior which conforms to adult norms.

Although McPhail avoids being prescriptive in his approach, he does draw certain conclusions about these responses. He feels that the mature-imaginative and experimental-sophisticated responses are "good" because they involve maximum consideration of other people's needs, feelings, and interests. On the other hand, aggressive responses are "bad" because they imply coercion without regard for the other person's basic concerns.

McPhail admits that it is more difficult to generalize about the other responses. Experimental-crude responses can be "bad" in their effect on others, but they indicate that the student is attempting to try out and learn from new forms of behavior. Mature-conventional responses are correct in the legal sense, but they may lack a deeper appreciation of an individual's needs. A dependent response indicates that the student relies on others to make his moral decisions. However, it could also indicate his willingness to consult others before making a decision, which, according to McPhail, is a sign of maturity and consideration.

Avoidance also can be interpreted in several ways. For example, it can be seen as a turning away from interpersonal problems. Conversely, in some situations it may be appropriate to avoid a confrontation if confrontation could lead to aggression.[8]

CONSEQUENCES.   The orientation in this unit is toward assessing the effects of actions on others and ourselves. "Probably most of us hurt people more frequently because we have not considered the possible consequences of our actions than because we are indifferent to others' interests, or wish to make them suffer."[9]

Thus the emphasis is on predicting the consequences of actions so that we can be aware of how they affect the needs and feelings of others. The consequences approach assumes that practicing this type of prediction will carry over to real life. McPhail feels that the group can be helpful in making predictions.

The group members can pool and share their ideas about what may happen and so become individually much more perceptive than they would be thinking in isolation. A further advantage is that group members can, generally without being conscious that they are doing so, support and help the rare boy or girl who is excessively concerned with the imagined destructive effects of his or her actions. There is plenty of opportunity to distinguish between what is probable and what is merely possible.[10]

The group context can also let the individual release aggressive feelings and discuss how such feelings can be dealt with constructively. The consequence orientation is complementary to the sensitivity materials, since sensitivity has been defined as "the ability to predict what an individual will say and do about you, himself and others."[11]

POINTS OF VIEW. This aspect of the sensitivity-consideration model focuses on developing empathy and understanding of another's viewpoint.

Classroom Application

The teaching process in the sensitivity-consideration model is both flexible and straightforward. The sensitivity materials, for example, can be used as follows:

1. Present the situation to the students.
2. Ask them to write down what they would do in the situation.
3. Ask for volunteers to present their solutions.
4. Role-play the solutions presented.
5. Discuss the solutions presented in the role playing.
6. Sum up and draw generalizations from the situation at hand. The different possible responses (e.g., dependent, conventional, aggressive) can also be presented and discussed.

For example, one situation that might be presented is the following: "You think that your father is being unreasonable and aggressive when you are arguing with him. What do you do?"[12] Some of the possible responses and the corresponding classifications are as follows:

Stop arguing. (Passive)

Stop arguing but feel in a ferment. (Passive-emotional)

Ask your mother for support. (Dependent-adult)

Talk to your friends about how awkward he is. (Dependent-peer)

Tell him a thing or two about what he can do. (Aggressive)

Thump him! (Very aggressive)

Keep out of his way whenever possible. (Avoidance)

Try and get him really worked up. (Experimental-crude)

Attempt to calm him dowm. (Experimental-sophisticated)

Tell him that you cannot discuss things with him if he loses his temper. (Mature-conventional)

Reason pleasantly with him while realizing that you may have to give it up if he doesn't calm down. (Mature-imaginative)[13]

The teacher should not introduce these responses too soon, however. There should be ample opportunity for the students to discuss and role-play alternative solutions.

The consequences teaching process involves the following steps, although steps 5 to 7 are optional:

1. Select a situation and write it on the board. For example: "Outline what could happen when someone removes a lifebuoy from a pier and plays with it."[14]
2. Ask the students to write down the short- and long-term effects of the action on people, the surrounding environment, and the actor. Sometimes the students can diagram the possible effects.
3. Have the students share their lists and diagrams.
4. Discuss the "realism," or feasibility, of the suggested outcomes.
5. Have students role-play consequences or even develop short one-act plays.
6. Encourage students to collect materials (newspapers, pictures, etc.) relevant to the situations.
7. Have students do some creative work, such as writing poems or painting pictures, related to the situation.

A few of the possible consequences of the lifebuoy situation are as follows:[15]

BOY WHO REMOVES LIFE-BUOY: leaves it lying about; loses it in a bed of nettles; puts it back later; is indifferent— never gives it a thought; worries about it.

AFTER TRAGIC CONSE-QUENCES: feels guilty, miserable and shocked; cannot forget what happened; wonders why no one told him of the dangers of playing with a lifebuoy or stopped him from removing it.

McPhail suggests that the following teaching approach can be applied to the points-of-view materials:

1. Present the situation. For example:

ELDERLY STAMMERER: (to the clerk in the Employment Exchange) I w-w-w-w-aaaant-t-t-t . . .
CLERK: Take it easy and get it out, Dad.

What do you think of the clerk's attitude?

What do you think it is like to stammer? [16]

2. Ask the students to write out or role-play what they would do in the situation.
3. Encourage students to take each person's role in the situation.
4. Open the discussion to consider alternative points of view.

The work-card situations represent a variety of conflicts. One set focuses on improving the ability to understand the needs and interests of the opposite sex. Another set concerns developing sensitivity to people of different generations. A third centers on conflicts between people occupying different class positions in society. A fourth concerns racial, cultural, and political conflict. A fifth set relates to conflicts arising from different psychological viewpoints.

This approach, then, focuses on specific conflicts to develop empathy and sensitivity. McPhail suggests that this aspect of the model also improves interpersonal relations in the school.

The Teachers's Role

The teacher must, of course, be sensitive to the needs and interests of the students. Otherwise there is little hope of developing consideration in them.

McPhail suggests that the teacher should keep things moving when using this model. If students' interest flags, future attempts to facilitate their sensitivity will be difficult. The model is flexible, since the materials can be used readily in small-group work. The model can also be a stimulus for creative work in writing, painting, and music.

McPhail emphasizes that developing sensitivity and empathy does not mean sacrificing one's own concerns or identity.

> **One should not make an exception in one's own case and act selfishly in disregard of others; conversely, no one should be expected to treat himself as less than a person. Apart from anything else, encouraging others to disregard your interest, to use you as a doormat, is not in their best interest: this is to confirm the selfish person in his selfishness, the neurotic in his neurosis.[17]**

The teacher should feel free to develop his own materials in conjunction with students. The students themselves can identify situations that can be used for discussion and role playing. Newspapers and magazines can also be introduced to stimulate sensitivity discussion.

Applicability of the Model

Because of its flexibility the model can be used in a variety of situations. However, it is designed primarily for secondary-school students.

Figure 11

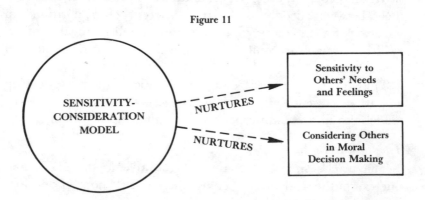

The Learning Environment

The sensitivity-consideration model is nurturant. In dealing with various situations sensitivity and consideration are gradually developed in the students.

TRANSACTIONAL ANALYSIS

Transactional analysis (TA) has become a popular method of analyzing interpersonal functioning. Recently, it has been applied to education and patterns of interaction within the classroom. Ken Ernst's book *Games Students Play* applies TA techniques to schools.

Theoretical Orientation

Four types of analysis are associated with TA. *Structural analysis* concerns the individual personality. *Transactional anaylsis* relates to what people do and say to one another. *Game analysis* focuses on transactions that lead to certain "payoffs." *Script analysis* concerns specific life dramas that individuals act out compulsively.

STRUCTURAL ANALYSIS. In order to understand transactional analysis and game analysis, one must be acquainted with the fundamentals of structural analysis.

Each individual has three ego states. Eric Berne, founder of TA and game analysis, defines an ego state as "a consistent pattern of feeling and experience directly related to a corresponding consistent pattern of behavior."[18] These states are Parent (P), Adult (A), and Child (C), and are often diagramed as follows:

The Parent ego state contains values and behaviors incorporated from outside sources, usually parents. The behaviors associated with this state are critical or nurturing. In fact, Berne refers to two separate Parent states—the Critical Parent and the Nurturing Parent.

The Adult ego state focuses on external reality and gathering information. This state has been compared to a computer, which receives information and organizes it rationally. The state is not related to a person's age; thus, a child can function in the Adult ego state.

The Child ego state contains the natural impulses of childhood as well as socialized responses to parental authority. It is thus referred to as the Natural Child, who is spontaneous and creative, or the Adapted Child, who acts in ways to please his parents.

Examples of responses to a situation from each of these three states are presented below:

TO A STIMULUS OF A PIECE OF MODERN ART:

PARENT: Good grief! What's it supposed to be!
ADULT: That costs $350 according to the price tag.
CHILD: Ooo, what pretty color!

TO A REQUEST FOR AN OFFICE REPORT:

PARENT: Mr. Brown is not cut out to be a supervisor.
ADULT: I know Mr. Brown needs these by five o'clock.
CHILD: No matter what I do I can't please Mr. Brown.[19]

TRANSACTIONAL ANALYSIS. Transactional analysis is concerned with interactions between the various ego states. Transactions can be classified as (1) complementary, (2) crossed, or (3) ulterior.

Complementary transactions involve messages from one ego state which are received by another person and returned in an expected manner. These are essentially open, healthy interactions. One of the goals of transactional analysis is to facilitate complementary transactions. The educational aim is to facilitate complementary transactions in the classroom between teacher and student and between student and student. Two examples of complementary transactions are as follows:

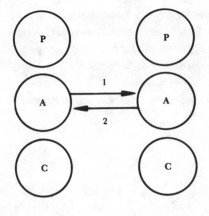

Data exchange in
Adult/Adult transaction

1. What time is it?
2. 3:30 P.M.

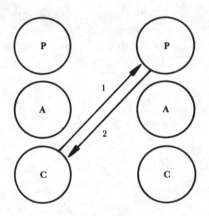

Exchange between
Child and Nurturing Parent

1. I'm not feeling well.
2. Perhaps you'd better
   stay inside today
   because it's cold out.

In a crossed transaction, one individual sends a message and another individual responds in an unexpected and noncomplementary way.

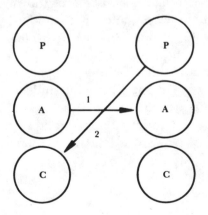

1. Student: What's our
   homework for tomorrow?
2. Teacher: Don't you
   ever listen?

The most complex transactions are ulterior since two ego states within the same person send messages, which often conflict. One message is sent orally, but there is a hidden message within, usually from another ego state. The hidden message can be conveyed verbally or nonverbally. For example, if the student submits a sloppy paper to the teacher, he may be asking for a parental putdown.

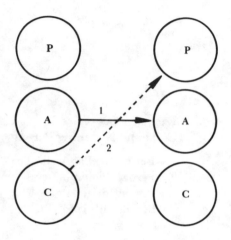

1. **Student submits sloppy paper.**
2. **Student: I want to be scolded.**

GAME ANALYSIS. The student in the previous diagram was involved in game playing. A psychological game is "a recurring set of transactions, often repetitive, superficially rational, with a concealed motivation; or, more colloquially, is a series of transactions with a gimmick."[20] Games hinder genuine, open communication since the motive is a "payoff." People play games to win, but in terms of personal integration they lose.

In *Games Students Play*, Ernst has identified a number of games found in schools. One is the game of "Uproar." Here the student attempts to disrupt the class through rebellious, Child behavior. For example, when the roll is called, Muriel attempts to create an uproar by responding to her name with a loud whine. It's supposed to be Mur-i-ELL."

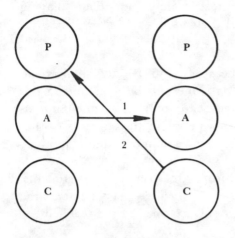

1. **Teacher: Is Muriel Mills here?**
2. **Student: It's supposed to be Mur-i-ELL.**

How the teacher responds to Muriel will determine whether the game continues.

SCRIPT ANALYSIS.   Often an individual will identify with certain Child ego states and will play out a life plan based on those states. James and Jongeward describe a person who plays the following life script:

> In counseling, Fred reported, "If I heard it once, I heard it a hundred times, 'What a stupid thing to do, Fred. Can't you do anything right?' I couldn't even talk fast enough for my folks, and I still stutter sometimes. When I went to school, I just couldn't seem to do anything right. I was always at the bottom of the class, and I can remember teachers saying, 'Fred, that was a stupid question.' Teachers were just like my mom. When they read the grades out loud, my name was last, and the kids laughed at me. Then I got to high school, and the counselor said I could do better. That I wasn't dumb, just lazy. I just don't get it."[21]

Fred's life script is "I'm not O.K., I'm stupid." Eventually Fred became conscious of this script and gave up his game of "Stupid."

The teacher who is aware of transactional analysis can "clean up" transactions within the classroom, facilitate healthy inter-

and intra-personal development, and help individuals playing dysfunctional life scripts to end their games and grow.

Classroom Application

Transactional analysis can be applied to the classroom at two levels. At one level, the teacher alone can be conscious of ego states and transactions and attempt to facilitate open communication. At another level, he can work with the students so that they themselves are aware of ego states, games, ulterior motives, and so on.

The first level might be appropriate with younger students. For example, in the situation described earlier involving the teacher and Muriel, several options are open to the teacher:

1. **Blow up and bawl out Muriel, as the Tyrant Teacher might.**
2. **Suffer in silence, as the Martyr Teacher might.**
3. **Feel hurt, as the Whining Teacher might.**
4. **Argue, as the Scrapping Teacher might.**
5. **Kick her out, as the Impatient Teacher might.**
6. **Fear her, as the Timid Teacher might.**
7. **Turn her game off by using . . . Transactional Analysis.**[22]

The last approach involves the following activities. The teacher can tell Muriel in a calm and firm Adult voice that she is to see him after school. If he speaks to Muriel in a Parent voice, he might further provoke her. After school, again in the Adult ego state, the teacher explains that his job is to help students learn and to prevent disruptions. He also tells her

> **that school is like a free supermarket. The student can go in, load up, and leave without paying because her parents have already paid. If Muriel does not like the grocery clerk she can get even with him by not taking the goodies or she can ignore her dislike for him and load up anyway.**[23]

The last step is to establish some sort of rapport so that communication can be continued. This will let the teacher give Muriel positive "strokes," or recognition, rather than the kind of negative stroking she seeks in "Uproar." The teacher can inquire and learn about any special interests (e.g., artwork) and thus continue communicating and giving positive strokes. He tries to let Muriel know that she is O.K. in a situation outside the "game" context.

In sum, the teacher engages in the following steps:

1. Diagnoses transactions and games in the classroom.
2. Finds the payoff to each game.
3. Resists the temptation to give the payoff to the game player. In short, doesn't use "Uproar" to deal with an "Uproar."
4. Gives the player appropriate strokes in another context before the game gets started. Lets the person know he is O.K. in a context outside the game.

Of course, the teacher should become aware of his own games. Games some teachers play include the "close to student" game, in which the teacher tries to be the student's buddy. Here the Child ego state of the teacher seeks strokes from the students. "I know best" is also a popular game with some teachers, as the teacher's Critical Parent becomes dominant.

At the secondary- and post-secondary-school level, the teacher can instruct the students in transactional analysis concepts and employ some TA activities that facilitate open communication and autonomy. In *Born to Win* James and Jongeward describe a number of activities that could be used in this way. For example, the following activity can be used to increase awareness of the various ego states.

> **Imagine you are at home alone on a stormy night. You've been asleep for several hours. The doorbell rings unexpectedly, and by the sound of the clock's striking you know that it is 3:00 A.M.**
> **What are your feelings and thoughts? What would you do?**
> **How would you have felt as a child? Do you feel this now?**
> **What would each of your parents have done? Would your behavior resemble that of one of your parent figures?**
> **What do you think is the "best" thing to do?**[24]

At this level the teaching process involves: (1) Instructing the students in basic TA concepts; (2) Presenting various activities to make the students aware of their own ego states, games, life scripts, and so on; and (3) Helping the students to end game playing and develop positive life scripts.

The Teacher's Role

The teacher using transactional analysis must, of course, be familiar with TA theory, and, preferably, have had some training and practice in a TA group. He should be aware of his own ego states and games and should work to "clean up" his games. Knowing the name of the game is not important, but it is important to be aware of transactions and avoid being caught in games with negative payoffs.

Applicability of the Model

The model is moderate to low in structure. It is applicable to a wide variety of situations because it can be used to analyze almost any type of transaction that occurs in the classroom at any level on the educational continuum. One of the possible limitations is that a teacher might see himself as a therapist and go too far with some of the TA techniques. The main value of these techniques for the classroom is in analyzing interactions between individuals, not in providing therapy to the students.

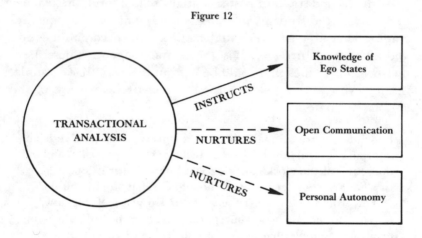

Figure 12

The Learning Environment

Transactional analysis is both instructional and nurturant. It can instruct the student about the different ego states and TA theory and nurture open communications and personal growth.

HUMAN RELATIONS TRAINING:
The T-group Method

The only constant today is change. Many people hold this view of society, and the human relations training method was designed to allow people to cope with change constructively. Industry began to use the Training Group, or T-group, in the 1950s, and many managers have made the trip to the National Training Laboratory at Bethel, Maine, where the T-group method was developed. More recently, teachers and educational administrators have been studying the T-group and its potential value to educational settings. Some educators suggest that the T-group is relevant to the training of teachers and administrators. The principal, for instance, can learn skills for developing a cooperative atmosphere in the school.

As a model of teaching, human relations training has the following student objectives:

1. A spirit of inquiry and willingness to experiment with one's role in the world.
2. An increased sensitivity to the behavior of others. This refers to the development of an awareness of voice inflections, facial expressions, and bodily positions, and of an ability to respond to these stimuli. The person gains a capacity for empathy.
3. Increased awareness of factors that facilitate or hinder group functioning.
4. The ability to intervene in a group situation to improve group functioning.
5. The ability to resolve conflict situations through problem solving rather than through coercion or manipulation.[25]

These goals are broad and are sometimes difficult to identify in terms of specific student behaviors. The training method itself is based on several assumptions:

1. In a group setting, individuals can give each other constructive feedback. Feedback means that the group members respond to each other's reactions and feelings in an open but descriptive way.
2. Psychological safety, or a sense of mutual trust, is necessary if the group is to be effective.
3. Anxiety facilitates new learning. Although a sense of mutual trust is necessary, a certain amount of ambiguity is also necessary to facilitate learning. If the setting is too structured, the participants will not be able to take risks and to try out new behaviors.

4. The learning that occurs within the group will transfer to other situations.[26]

Classroom Application

The T-group method is unstructured. The method employs a small face-to-face group in which the focus is on the here-and-now. The members discuss themselves and how they are acting in the context of the group. The group leader attempts to set an example for this here-and-now focus and the giving and receiving of effective feedback. Feedback is essential to this process, since it is through feedback that learning occurs.

Feedback is useful when:

1. It describes what [a person] is doing rather than placing a value on it. Example: "When you yell at me it makes me feel like not talking to you any more." Rather than: "It's awful of you to yell at me."
2. It is specific rather than general.
3. It is directed toward behavior which the receiver can do something about.
4. It is well-timed.
5. It is asked for rather than imposed.
6. It is checked to insure clear communication.[27]

In order for feedback to occur there must be a certain amount of anxiety in the group. This anxiety is not excessive but serves to break the student from his preconceived notions and repetitive behavior patterns. Each participant should be "clean" in his relations. That is, he should not play games—activities in which the players feel "put down" because one of the participants is manipulative.

Although a certain amount of anxiety is involved, the group must also have a sense of psychological safety. This means that the group supports each member in experimenting with new behaviors and being open with feelings. In short, there must be a basic sense of trust among the members or the T-group will be dysfunctional. The trainer again is a key element in that he must absorb feelings and be supportive of the expression of feelings in others. If the trainer is perceived as nonsupportive, then the group will not function effectively.

A handbook has been prepared which outlines a number of T-group activities for the classroom.[28] An example is "Decision by Consensus," developed by NASA.

DECISION BY CONSENSUS

INSTRUCTIONS: This is an exercise in group decision making. Your group is to employ the method of GROUP CONSENSUS in reaching its decision. This means that the prediction for each of the 15 survival items must be agreed upon by each group member before it becomes a part of the group decision. Consensus is difficult to reach. Therefore, not every ranking will meet with everyone's complete approval. Try, as a group, to make each ranking one with which all group members can at least partially agree. Here are some guides to use in reaching consensus:

1. Avoid arguing for your own individual judgments. Approach the task on the basis of logic.
2. Avoid changing your mind only in order to reach agreement and avoid conflict. Support only solutions with which you are able to agree somewhat, at least.
3. Avoid "conflict-reducing" techniques such as majority vote, averaging, or trading in reaching decisions.
4. View differences of opinion as helpful rather than as a hindrance in decision making.

On the "Group Summary Sheet" place the individual rankings made earlier by each group member. Take as much time as you need in reaching your group decision.

Instructions

You are a member of a space crew originally scheduled to rendezvous with a mother ship on the lighted surface of the moon. Due to mechanical difficulties, however, your ship was forced to land at a spot some 200 miles from the rendezvous point. During reentry and landing, much of the equipment aboard was damaged and, since survival depends on reaching the mother ship, the most critical items available must be chosen for the 200-mile trip. Below are listed the 15 items left intact and undamaged after landing. Your task is to rank-order them in terms of their importance for your crew in allowing them to reach the rendezvous point. Place the number 1 by the most important item, the number 2 by the second most important, and so on through number 15, the least important.

Boxes of matches   _____

Food concentrate   _____

50 ft. of nylon rope   _____

Parachute silk   _____

Portable heating unit   _____

Two .45 caliber pistols   _____

One case dehydrated Pet Milk   _____

Two 100 lb. tanks of oxygen   _____

Stellar map (of moon's constellation)   _____

Life raft   _____

Magnetic compass   _____

Signal flares   _____

First-aid kit containing injection needles   _____

Solar-powered FM receiver-transmitter   _____

5 gallons of water   _____

Scoring Instructions for Decision by Consensus

The prediction is that the group product will be more accurate than the average for the individuals. The lower the score, the more accurate. A score of "0" is a perfect score.

Each individual can score his own sheet. As you read aloud to the group the correct rank for each item, they simply take the difference between their rank and the correct rank on that item and write it down. Do this for each item and add up these differences. DISREGARD " + " and " − ."

To get the average for all individuals, divide the sum of the individual scores by the number of individuals in the group. Compute the group score in the same way you computed each of the individual scores. If our hypothesis is correct, the group score will be lower than the average for all individuals.

Possible Questions for the Group

1. Did the group really go by consensus? Or did we gloss over conflicts?

2. Did the group stay on the intellectual or task aspects or did we stop to examine our process to see how we could work more effectively?

3. How satisfied were we with the way the group worked?

How efficient were we?

1   9

very poor   excellent

4. How satisfied are you (as members) with the group?

5. How much influence did you feel you had as an individual on the group decision?

6. Did the group listen to you? Ignore you?

7. Did you stay involved in the exercise or did you give up?

8. In what ways could you change or improve your interaction with others?

GROUP SUMMARY SHEET

Individual Predictions

	1	2	3	4	5	6	7	8	9	10	11	Group Prediction
Box of matches												
Food concentrate												
50 ft. of nylon rope												
Parachute silk												
Portable heating unit												
Two .45 cal. pistols												
One case dehydrated milk												
Two tanks oxygen												
Stellar map												
Life raft												
Magnetic compass												

	1	2	3	4	5	6	7	8	9	10	11	Group Prediction
Signal flares												
First-aid kit w/needles												
Solar-powered radio												
5 gallons of water												

KEY

Little or no use on moon	15 Box of matches
Supply daily food required	4 Food concentrate
Useful in tying injured together, help in climbing	6 50 ft. nylon rope
Shelter against sun's rays	8 Parachute silk
Useful only if party landed on dark side	13 Portable heating unit
Self-propulsion devices could be made from them	11 Two .45 caliber pistols
Food, mixed with water for drinking	12 Dehydrated Pet Milk
Fills respiration requirement	1 Two tanks of oxygen
A principal means of finding directions	3 Stellar map
CO_2 bottles for self-propulsion across chasms, etc.	9 Life raft
Probably no magnetic poles; useless	14 Magnetic compass
Distress call when line of sight possible	10 Signal flares
Oral pills or injection medicine valuable	7 First-aid kit with injection needles

Distress-signal transmitter, possible communication with mother ship	5	Solar-powered FM receiver-transmitter
Replenishes loss from sweating, etc.	2	Five gallons of water

After this activity the students assess how the group functions and how each individual facilitates group problem solving. This can be done through the use and understanding of group functions. These functions have been grouped into two overall areas: helping functions and hindering functions.[29] Hindering functions include four activities:

1. Seeking recognition: Calling attention to oneself through unusual behavior such as telling stories, boasting, and loud talking.
2. Digressing: Getting away from the topic or the group task.
3. Out of field: Withdrawing from the discussion.
4. Blocking: Interfering with the group task by arguing excessively or by continually bringing up a "dead" issue.

The helping functions are divided into two subgroups. Some functions are related to the group task and others are concerned with maintaining and developing the proper emotional climate. Task functions are:

1. Initiating: Proposing and defining the task for the group.
2. Seeking information or opinions: Asking questions about relevant information; or asking for expression of feelings or personal value.
3. Giving information or opinion: Offering relevant information; stating opinion or expressing personal value.
4. Summarizing: Bringing ideas together so that the group can refocus on the problem; offering a conclusion that the group can accept or reject.
5. Clarifying: Clearing up misunderstanding; defining terminology; rephrasing a statement to facilitate understanding.
6. Consensus testing: Checking with the group to see whether they are reaching a decision.

Maintenance functions include:

1. Encouraging: Supporting other group members; indicating through nonverbal gestures acceptance of another's thoughts.
2. Harmonizing: Trying to reconcile disagreements; reducing the anxiety level.
3. Compromising: Willing to yield status or admit error so that the group can function.
4. Gate keeping: Keeping channels of communication open; asking others to participate; suggesting procedures that allow others to participate.
5. Standard-setting: Exploring whether group members are satisfied with procedures.

Often these functions can be used in an inner- and outer-circle situation. Some students sit in the inside circle and discuss a problem, while other students sit on the outside and record how the individuals in the inner circle helped or hindered group functioning. Students in the outer circle can use a chart to indicate how students on the inner circle are performing the various func-

Table 4

TASK FUNCTIONS	A	B	C	D	E	F	G	H	I	J	K	L	M	N
1. Initiating														
2. Seeking information														
3. Giving information														
4. Summarizing														
5. Clarifying														
6. Consensus testing														
MAINTENANCE FUNCTIONS														
1. Encouraging														
2. Harmonizing														
3. Compromising														
4. Gate keeping														
5. Standard-setting														
HINDERING FUNCTIONS														
1. Seeking recognition														
2. Digressing														
3. Out of field														
4. Blocking														

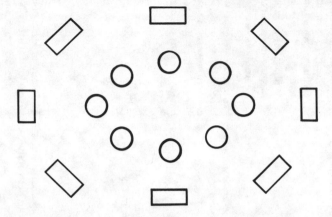

tions. The data collected by the outer circle then can be used in giving feedback to the students in the inner circle.

The Teacher's Role

As mentioned earlier, a teacher should give and receive feedback and also facilitate a climate of psychological safety. The teacher does not dominate the situation but models behavior related to effective group functioning. In the classroom situation he can make use of several of the activities that are available for analyzing group behavior. However, there are certain conditions that prevent the classroom from becoming a pure T-group. For example, some individuals suggest that the T-group is most effective in an isolated setting with people who are strangers. These conditions do not apply to the secondary-school classroom. Similarly, most T-groups are small as compared to a class of thirty to forty students. Finally, most T-groups are short in duration compared with the length of most secondary-school courses.[30] Still, these items do not mean that the teacher can't use some of the strategies associated with the model. He can still model feedback procedures and create a climate of mutual support. The teacher can also use activities like the inner and outer circle and the decision-by-consensus exercise.

Since the T-group is generally unstructured, it is most appropriate for high CL students. Some of the exercises, however, are moderately structured and could be used with medium CL students. In sum, the T-group method helps students gain skills in

SUMMARY: SENSITIVITY AND GROUP ORIENTATION

	Communications Training	Sensitivity-Consideration	Transactional Analysis	Human Relations Training
Aims	Skills in empathy, genuineness, respect, specificity, confrontation, immediacy, and self-disclosure	Sensitivity to another person's needs and feelings	Open communications and personal growth	1. Skills in diagnosing and skillfully intervening to facilitate group functioning 2. Willingness to experiment with one's role 3. Learning how to learn
Teaching Process	1. Teacher determines grouping pattern 2. Helpee states problem 3. Helper responds, using scales to shape responses 4. Group members rate helper response	This varies with the subprocess (e.g., sensitivity, consequences, and points of view) but generally involves the following steps: 1. Present situation 2. Allow student to develop response 3. Discuss or role-play situation and responses 4. Draw generalizations from role playing and discussion	1. Diagnose transactions in the classroom 2. Find payoff to each game 3. Resist giving payoff to game player 4. Give player positive strokes in another context	Process is emergent, with here-and-now focus. Teacher may, however, use exercises and then analyze behavior patterns during exercise
Teacher's Role	Model communication skills	Model sensitivity and keep process moving	Develop open climate and avoid initiating destructive games	Maintain an atmosphere of psychological safety, yet also create enough ambiguity to "unfreeze" behavior patterns
Amount of Structure	High	Moderate	Moderate to Low	Low, with exercises in moderate range

group interaction. It can be used in the classroom, but the teacher must recognize its limitations.

Applicability of the Model

This method is most relevant to secondary- and post-secondary-school settings. In its pure form it would have limited applicability, but many of the exercises and some of the main features of the model (i.e., giving and receiving feedback) can be integrated into the ongoing life of the classroom.

The Learning Environment

The low structure of the human relations training model provides a learning environment that is nurturant. The model facilitates sensitivity to others, group interaction skills, and the ability to cope with change and ambiguity.

Figure 13

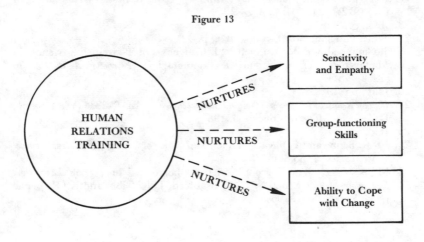

Notes

1. Carl Rogers, "Toward Becoming a Fully Functioning Person," *Perceiving, Behaving, Becoming,* Association for Supervision and Curriculum Development Yearbook (Washington, D.C.: National Education Association, 1962), p. 31.
2. R. R. Carkhuff, *Helping and Human Relations* (New York: Holt, Rinehart & Winston, 1969), vol. 2, pp. 315–28.
3. D. N. Aspy, "A Study of Three Facilitative Conditions and Their Relationships to the Achievement of Third-Grade Students." Unpublished doctoral dissertation, University of Kentucky, 1965.
4. Carkhuff, vol. 1, p. 219.

5. Carkhuff, vol. 2, pp. 143–45. (Reprinted with permission.)
6. Peter McPhail, *In Other People's Shoes* (London: Longmans, 1972), p. 10.
7. Ibid., p. 13.
8. Ibid., pp. 8–9.
9. Ibid., p. 42.
10. Ibid., pp. 42–43.
11. Ibid., p. 45.
12. Ibid., p. 13.
13. Ibid., p. 20.
14. Ibid., p. 56.
15. Ibid.
16. Ibid., p. 82.
17. Ibid., p. 62.
18. Eric Berne, *Principles of Group Treatment* (New York: Oxford University Press, 1964), p. 364.
19. Muriel James and Dorothy Jongeward, *Born to Win: Transactional Analysis with Gestalt Experiments* (Reading, Mass.: Addison-Wesley, 1973), p. 19.
20. Eric Berne, "Transactional Analysis," in *Active Psychotherapy,* edited by Harold Greenwald (New York: Atherton Press, 1967), p. 125.
21. James and Jongeward, *Born to Win,* pp. 38–39.
22. Ken Ernst, *Games Students Play* (Millbrae, Calif.: Celestial Arts Publishing Co., 1972), p. 19.
23. Ibid., p. 27.
24. James and Jongeward, *Born to Win,* p. 42.
25. J. Campbell and M. Dunnette, "Effectiveness of T-group Experiences in Management Training and Development," in *Psychological Bulletin* 70 (1968): 75.
26. Ibid., p. 77.
27. *Human Relations Laboratory Training Student Notebook,* ED 018834 (Washington, D.C.: U.S. Office of Education, 1961).
28. Ibid.
29. K. R. Benne and P. Sheats, "Functional Roles of Group Members," *Journal of Social Issues* 4, no. 2 (1948).
30. M. B. Miles, "The T-group and the Classroom," in *T-group Theory and Laboratory Method,* edited by L. P. Bradford, J. R. Gibb, and K. R. Benne (New York: Wiley, 1964).

OTHER MODELS AND BIBLIOGRAPHY

Other Models

Group Investigation Model
Developed by Herbert Thelen, this model instructs the student to inquire in an academic area and acquire interpersonal skills, and also nurtures interpersonal warmth and affiliation. See Herbert Thelen, *Education and the Human Quest* (New York: Harper & Row, 1960).

Jurisprudential Model
This approach also facilitates sensitivity to another person's values, but within a strong analytic framework that focuses on controversial issues. Developed by Don Oliver, James Shaver, and Fred Newmann, materials are available through Public Issues Series/Harvard Social Studies Project.

Teacher Effectiveness Training
Developed by Thomas Gordon, this model facilitates communication skills. See Thomas Gordon, *T.E.T: Teacher Effectiveness Training* (New York: Peter Weyden, 1974).

Bibliography

Berne, Eric. *Games People Play: The Psychology of Human Relations.* New York: Grove Press 1964 (paperback). Although originally written for a professional audience, this work has become a best-seller.

Carkhuff, R. R. *Helping and Human Relations,* volumes 1 & 2. New York: Holt, Rinehart & Winston, 1969. Provides a comprehensive overview of communications training. The reader may find that the jargon gets in the way of the overall presentation.

Ernst, Ken. *Games Students Play.* Millbrae, Calif.: Celestial Arts Publishing Co., 1972. Ernst studied with Berne, who asked him to apply the techniques of TA to schools. This book is the result of that request. A number of specific student and teacher games are explained as well.

Harris, Thomas A. *I'm OK—You're OK: A Practical Guide to Transactional Analysis.* New York: Harper & Row, 1969. The layman's guide to transactional analysis.

Human Relations Laboratory Training Student Notebook, ED 018834. Washington, D.C.: U.S. Office of Education, 1961. Developed at Springport High School in Michigan, this handbook provides a number of exercises that can be used in the secondary school.

James, Muriel, and Jongeward, Dorothy. *Born to Win: Transactional Analysis with Gestalt Experiments.* Reading, Mass.: Addison-Wesley, 1973. An easy-to-read overview of transactional analysis, presented with a number of interesting exercises, some of which could be used in the classroom.

McPhail, Peter. *Lifeline.* London: Longmans, 1972. *In Other People's Shoes* is the first part of this series. The other two parts—*Proving the Rule* and *What Would You Have Done?*—provide a number of case studies for discussion.

McPhail, Peter; Ungoed-Thomas, J. R.; and Chapman, Hilary. *Moral Education in the Secondary Schools.* London: Longmans, 1972. Provides the theoretical framework for the Schools Council Project in Moral Education and the *Lifeline* series.

Miles, M. B. "The T-group and the Classroom," in *T-group Theory and Laboratory Method,* edited by L. P. Bradford, J. R. Gibb, and K. R. Benne. New York: Wiley, 1964. A sensible article discussing the limitations of applying the T-group to the classroom.

CHAPTER 6
CONSCIOUSNESS EXPANSION

Try the following exercise. Close your eyes and attempt to sense each side of your body separately. Try to get in touch with the feelings of the left and of the right side, their strengths, their weaknesses. When you are finished, open your eyes for a moment and reflect on one of these questions. Close your eyes and sense inside for the answer, then repeat the process with the next question.

1. Which side of you is more feminine?
2. Which is more masculine?
3. Which do you consider the "dark" side of yourself?
4. Which side is the "lighter"?
5. Which is more active?
6. Which is more passive?
7. Which side is more logical?
8. Which more "intuitive"?
9. Which side of you is the more mysterious?
10. Which side is the more artistic?[1]

If you are right-handed, you probably sense that the right side of your body is more logical, active, lighter, and masculine. In most people these sensations reflect the two sides of the brain, since there is now enough neurological evidence to support the assertion that the brain consists of two distinct hemispheres, each responsible for a different mode of consciousness.

The left side of the brain, which is related to the right side of the body, is responsible for analytic thought. It operates in a linear fashion and processes information sequentially. Such activities as language and mathematics depend on this mode of consciousness.

The right side of the brain, which is related to the left side of the body, operates in holistic fashion. Instead of viewing life in a linear, sequential fashion, this side of the brain sees things in terms of the total gestalt. This sphere is responsible for perceiving spatial relations, for artistic endeavors, and for recognizing faces.

Ideally, the two modes of consciousness complement each other. The process of building a house provides an example of the complementary nature of the modes.

> At first, there may be a sudden inspiration of the gestalt of the finished house, but this image must be brought to completion slowly, by linear methods, by plans and contracts, and then by the actual construction, sequentially, piece by piece.[2]

Robert Assagioli, the founder of psychosynthesis, suggests how intellect and intuition can complement each other.

> We will consider intuition mainly in its cognitive function—i.e., as a psychic organ or means to apprehend reality. It is a synthetic function in the sense that it apprehends the totality of a given situation or psychological reality. It does not work from the part to the whole—as the analytical mind does—but apprehends a totality directly in its living existence. . . .
> Intuition is the creative advance toward reality. Intellect [needs first to perform] the valuable and necessary function of interpreting—i.e., of translating, verbalizing in acceptable mental terms—the results of the intuition; second, to check its validity; and third, to coordinate and to include it into the body of already accepted knowledge. . . . A really fine and harmonious interplay between the two can work perfectly in a successive rhythm: intuitional insight, interpretation, further insight and its interpretation, and so on.[3]

Except for a few subject areas, such as art and English, most school curriculums have ignored the intuitive half of human consciousness. The approaches discussed in this chapter try to tune into this aspect of human consciousness.

Meditation is one approach. Through concentrating visually on an object such as a candle flame or repeating a word or mantra such as *om*, the student develops intuitive awareness. The student also can learn meditative methods that open his consciousness to deeper levels of himself and to his environment.

Synectics is designed to increase the student's creative and imaginative capacities. Through metaphor, the individual can create something new or deepen his understanding of an academic subject area.

Confluent education uses a number of activities to integrate the cognitive and the affective. The confluent model also stresses the integration of body and mind and includes exercises in sensory awareness to facilitate this unity.

Psychosynthesis includes a variety of techniques that allow the student to come in touch with his intuitive center or "Higher Self." Through this center the person can become aware of conflicting elements in his personality and consciousness and synthesize them into an integrated whole.

The consciousness-expansion models range from high to low in structure. Most meditation exercises are structured activities, while synectics is moderately structured because of teacher direction. Confluent education and psychosynthesis are generally low in structure, although a number of exercises associated with these models are moderately structured.

MEDITATION

For years, meditation was popularly viewed in the West as a strange mystical activity practiced only by yogis in the mountains of Tibet. Recently, however, meditation has become widely practiced here. Many individuals have begun meditating to become more aware and to come into contact with their Higher Self. Controlled studies have indicated a number of other benefits as well. For example, individuals who meditate breathe less rapidly and become less anxious.[4] A study of meditating high-school students indicated that the practice increased their self-esteem, energy, and tolerance and decreased their anxiety and tendency to conform.[5]

Robert Ornstein, a psychologist, has discussed forms of meditation in a manner that could be classified as a teaching model. In brief, he has articulated the theoretical background for meditation and identified a number of specific practices that could be used in the classroom.

In The Psychology of Consciousness, Ornstein relates meditation to the two modes of human consciousness.

> The concept "meditation" refers to a set of techniques which are the product of another type of psychology, one that aims at personal rather than intellectual knowledge. As such, the exercises are designed to produce an alteration in consciousness—a shift away from the active, outward-oriented, linear mode and toward the receptive and quiescent mode, and usually a shift from an external focus of attention to an internal one.[6]

Through meditation, it is claimed, an individual can activate the right-hemisphere mode of consciousness and thus develop his intuition and perception.

Classroom Application

Ornstein suggests that there are two basic approaches to meditation. Some exercises attempt to reduce stimuli so that the individual can focus attention on a particular object or on the repetition of a word. On the other hand, there are "opening-up" exercises that increase awareness of the external environment.

CONCENTRATIVE MEDITATION.   In this form of meditation the student shuts himself off from the outside world and concentrates on a particular object or sound. He tries to develop "one-pointed" consciousness, or the ability to focus attention on a single object. Although concentrative meditation takes several forms, the common element is one-pointedness.

Buddhist meditation.   This type of meditation is often begun with an exercise in which the student counts his intakes of breath from one to ten and then repeats the process. If he loses count, he begins counting again. After the student is able to concentrate on his breaths through counting, he can simply focus his attention on the process of breathing, observing the movement of air going in and out of his body. A sample set of instructions for this meditation follows:

> Sit in an upright, yet comfortable position. You may close your eyes or keep them open. If you keep your eyes open, fix them on a spot on the floor two or three feet in front of you.
> Don't force your breath but breathe slowly. Inhale slowly and

as you exhale count "one." Inhale slowly and again as you exhale count "two." Count the breaths to ten, then start with one
again.

Concentrate on the counting. If thoughts intervene, note them
and then gently return to the process of breathing and counting.
Don't attempt to push alien thoughts away, but simply focus on
the counting.

If you become anxious or uncomfortable, note the anxiety or
discomfort. Do not get lost in discomfort or comfort but merely
note and accept these states with similar compassion.

Research has indicated that this particular exercise assists
counselors in being integrated and more sensitive to the needs of
others.[7]

Yogic meditation.   There are several forms of yogic meditation.
One of the forms uses a *mantra,* simply a word or phrase the
student repeats continuously. The mantra can be said out loud in
a group setting, or the student can repeat it silently to himself.
The student focuses on the phrase, and if other thoughts intervene he gently returns his attention to the mantra. One example
of a mantra is *om.* The Buddhist phrase *om mani padme hum* is
another. Transcendental meditation (TM), which has become
popular in the West, uses the mantra. In TM the individual sits
in a comfortable position without assuming any special posture
and repeats the mantra. Like other forms of meditation, TM can
lead to a state in which the individual is deeply relaxed but also
very alert and conscious.

There has been much research indicating the positive effects of
mantra meditation. One study showed that individuals who
practiced mantra were more inner-directed and able to express
feelings in a more spontaneous way. Another study, which measured galvanic skin responses (GSR), suggests that meditators
experience less anxiety.[8]

Another form of yogic meditation is visual concentration, often
on an object or an image called a *mandala.* The mandala may be
just a simple circle so that attention gradually focuses on the
center of the circle. Or the mandala can be complex and intri-
cate in design. A popular visualization technique is to fix the
gaze on a candle flame. The aim of visual concentration is to
develop one-pointed consciousness.

Ornstein suggests that all concentrative techniques, although different in form, lead to the same goal because of their similar effect on the nervous system.

> This may indicate that one primary effect of the concentrative meditation exercises is the state of emptiness, the nonresponsiveness to the external world, evoked in the central nervous system by the continuous subroutine called up by the exercise, regardless of what the specific input is or what sensory modality is employed. Since we, the Bushmen, the Eskimos, the monks of Tibet, the Zen masters, the Yoga adepts, and the Dervishes all have the same kind of nervous system, it is not so surprising that similarities in techniques should have evolved.[9]

OPENING-UP MEDITATION EXERCISES.   These exercises ask the student to be aware of the here and now. Often our thoughts take us away from the present. Instead of attending fully to the activities at hand, we become lost in thoughts and imaginings. As a result, we may not listen to another person, or we may even become the victim of a traffic accident through our lack of attention to the present moment.

One exercise that attempts to develop the quality of being present is called "Now I Am Aware." First the student opens his senses to the external environment and states what he sees and hears. In the following illustration, Carl is being guided by his friend, Ron

> CARL: Now I look around this room. I see your desk. Now I see the clock. It's slow, no?
> RON: Stay in the now.
> CARL: Sorry.
> RON: Now I . . .
> CARL: Now I see the poster on the wall. Now I see a smudge on that poster. Now I see a tear in the corner. I think I did that. (Catches self.) Now I hear the clock.[10]

This procedure can be followed by exercises in which the student focuses on awareness of his body sensations and then his emotions.

Another opening-up meditation exercise is "Witness." Developed in yoga, "Witness" is a continuous exercise in which the student attempts to view himself and his actions objectively. The student notices everything that he does, but the Witness does not judge his actions or thoughts. Rahula describes the process.

Another very important, practical, and useful form of "meditation" (mental development) is to be aware and mindful of whatever you do, physically or verbally, during the daily routine of work in your life, private, public, or professional. Whether you walk, stand, sit, lie down or sleep, whether you stretch or bend your limbs, whether you look around, whether you put on your clothes, whether you talk or keep silent, whether you eat or drink—even whether you answer the calls of nature—in these and other activities you should be fully aware and mindful of the act performed at the moment.[11]

Another opening-up method is dishabituation. Here the student shifts his routine slightly to gain more awareness. For example, he eats with his left hand (if he is right-handed) to heighten his consciousness during eating. Other examples of dishabituation exercises are putting on shoes in the reverse order from usual or taking a slightly different route to school. In general, these opening-up exercises heighten an individual's awareness of himself and his environment.

The teaching process in meditation is straightforward. The teacher introduces the exercise, the student practices the meditation, and discussion can follow the practice period.

The Teacher's Role

In order to facilitate the student's ability to meditate, the teacher should have practiced some of the methods. Since the aim of meditation is to develop one-pointedness and a calm center within oneself, the teacher should have attained these qualities to some degree. It is useful to begin meditation with a short (5 to 10 minutes) period of practice and then gradually lengthen the practice time. A given meditation technique may or may not be suitable for a particular person. Some students feel comfortable with mantra, others find the Buddhist methods useful. The teacher should encourage each student to find a technique that is comfortable for him or her. Once comfortable with a method, the student should be encouraged to remain with that method.

Applicability of the Model

Because of their simplicity and structure, meditation techniques have potential use in many settings. However, since meditation practice in schools is relatively new, teachers may feel uncomfortable with the techniques, and this may limit their ap-

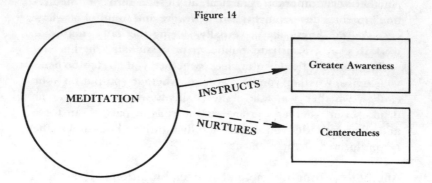

Figure 14

plicability. It should be stressed that the teacher must feel comfortable with meditation before introducing it into the curriculum. Like most of the affective education approaches, the models should be treated not as a collection of techniques or gimmicks but as vehicles for the facilitation of personal integration.

The Learning Environment

Meditation as a model of teaching is nurturant and instructional. First, meditation instructs the individual to be more aware and more conscious through the structured exercises. Meditation also gradually nurtures a sense of centeredness.

SYNECTICS

Synectics is a moderately structured approach that develops the individual's imaginative and creative capacities. Initially synectics was used in industry, but in recent years, William J. J. Gordon has developed a number of synectics materials for classroom use.

Assumptions and Theoretical Framework

Gordon argues that imagination and creativity can be dealt with consciously. Synectics assumes that the creative process is not a mysterious activity but can be observed and analyzed. Further, the creative process is the same whether applied to the arts or to science. Creativity and imagination always involve similar intellectual processes.

Another assumption is that creativity and imagination can be developed in a group setting. The group can stimulate the individual's imagination and creative capacities by providing emotional and intellectual diversity.

An important element in the creative process is the nonrational or emotional element. Gordon argues that the emotional is in fact more important than the rational in the creative process. Although the solutions to problems may be logical, the process of arriving at those solutions is not. However, the nonrational is also subject to analysis. It can be observed and understood and eventually integrated into conscious action.

The key to synectics training is the use of metaphor, which allows the student to *make the familiar strange* and to *make the strange familiar.* William Harvey's discovery of circulation is an example of Making the Familiar Strange.

In the sixteenth century, people thought that blood flowed from the heart to the body, surging in and out like the tides of the sea. Harvey was FAMILIAR with this view and believed it till he closely observed a fish's heart that was still beating after the fish had been opened up. He expected a tidal flow of blood, but he was reminded of a pump. The idea of the heart acting like a pump was most STRANGE to him and he had to break his ebb-and-flow connection to make room for his new pump connection. HE MADE THE FAMILIAR STRANGE.[12]

This is also a good example of how the creative process is applicable to science as well as the arts. Today, however, the student observing the fish's heart is involved in a different process. If the concept of the heart as a pump has just been explained to the student and thus is relatively strange, he needs to make the concept more familiar. "Where Harvey had to break his conception of the ebb-and-flow mechanism, the student has to only make a learning connection."[13] This connection might be made through the analogy of a swimming pool, where "dirty water is pumped through the filter and back to the pool."[14] The student can easily make the link between the heart and the water pump. He can also see how "the lungs and liver act as 'filters' when they cleanse the blood."[15] In brief, he makes the strange familiar through an analogy.

Gordon asserts that there are three types of analogies useful in synectics: direct analogy, personal analogy, and compressed conflict.

A *direct analogy* is a simple comparison of two objects or concepts. The analogy of the heart and water pump is a direct one. Another example is "A crab walks sideways like a sneaky burglar."[16] Direct analogies can be very close or they can be distant and somewhat strained.

In general, five levels of strain can separate an inorganic:inorganic comparison from an inorganic:organic one. For instance, a wheel of a car can be compared to the following objects that rotate as they move:
1. the cutter on a can opener;
2. the rotor of a helicopter;
3. the orbit of Mars;
4. a spinning seed pod;
5. a hoop snake.[17]

The first analogy is a close parallel since both objects are rotating, circular, metallic, and man-made. The last analogy is the most strained because a snake is a consciously moving animal rather than a man-made, inanimate object. Not everyone will agree with these conclusions, but the discussion and exploration of analogies are part of the creative process. Metaphors are not meant to represent substantive knowledge. But they can enliven one's relationship with knowledge in a more direct and personal way.

Personal analogies involve identification with inanimate or animate objects. Here there is more immediate and personal involvement with the object than in the direct analogy. Gordon asserts that there are four levels of personal analogy. At the first level there is merely a description of facts. For example, if asked to imagine himself as a fiddler crab, a student responding at the first level might say, "I would be hard on the outside because of my shell, and soft on the inside. I would have special little creases on my claws to grip and tear things, and one of my claws is twice as big as the other."[18] Here the individual does not identify with the object but merely describes the object. Students often state a personal analogy in this way when starting synectics.

The second level of personal analogy is first-person descriptions of emotions. Responding to the same question about the crab, the student at this level might say:

"I would be pretty busy getting food for myself, but I've got to be careful not to be food for a big fish. I've got to be careful not to get caught, but I must take some chances or the other crabs will beat me to it and I'll starve."[19]

Here the student begins to identify with the object, but in a minimal way.

The third level involves empathic identification with a living thing. Responding to the question about the crab at this level, the student might answer:

"O.K. I'm a fiddler crab. I've got armor all around me—my tough shell. You'd think I could take it easy, but I can't. And that big claw of mine! Big deal! It looks like a great weapon, but it's a nuisance. I wave it around to scare everyone, but I can hardly carry it. Why can't I be big and fast and normal like other crabs? No kidding! That claw doesn't even scare anyone!"[20]

This student is becoming more involved with the object. He is not just describing the object; he now identifies in an original way with the crab.

The fourth level of personal analogy involves empathic identification with a nonliving object. This requires the most imagination and empathy. An example of this type of identification occurs as follows:

TEACHER: Harold, imagine that you are the mud in which the fiddler crab makes his home.

STUDENT: I have the feeling that no one cares if I'm here or not. I'm full of holes into which the crabs crawl at night. They never thank me. I'm mud; that's all. I'd like to do something to make the crabs thank me. After all, if it were not for me, those crabs would get eaten up in one night.[21]

Compressed conflict, the third form of analogy, contains two words that don't seem to go together. For instance, "imprisoned freedom" is a compressed-conflict description of cellophane tape. This developed from personal analogies in which students developed the following thoughts:

"I feel as though I'm in prison. I am imprisoned glue, imprisoned potential. My glue is imprisoned inside me."

"I feel that potentially I am very useful, but when I'm free for use—pulled out in a strip and free, that is—then I feel that I offer only one level of freedom. If I am glue, then I'm so free to use that it takes real art to know how to use me, because I'm so free that I flow all over, and I am uncontrollable except by an expert."[22]

Scientists have used compressed conflict in developing their hypotheses. Before he discovered antitoxin, Louis Pasteur began to talk of "safe attack." Because of the surprise factor, compressed conflict can be the most powerful of the three metaphors.

Classroom Applications

The two basic teaching processes involved in synectics are making the strange familiar and making the familiar strange. The former involves gaining understanding of new information or a new concept. The latter focuses on producing something new or developing a more creative product. Making the strange familiar is concerned with making connections; making the familiar strange with breaking connections.

Making the strange familiar involves the following steps:

1. information input;
2. use of analogies to deepen understanding of the information or the concept;
3. refocusing on the information in light of the analogies.

In the following example, students who have read about Socrates are asked to think about his trial and death through the metaphoric process.

TEACHER: We have read the Dialogues and know Socrates drank the hemlock after being found guilty of treason and corrupting the youth of Athens. Why was he judged guilty? It's clear it was a frame-up to some extent.

JIM: We might ask how Socrates was viewed by the Athenians. How was Socrates viewed by his culture?

TEACHER: Let's take "culture" as a key word. Give an example of culture in the plant world.

CARL: How about fungus?

BETSY: . . . or a little place in the woods, like under a tree where there is a miniature garden in which the fungus and maybe a toadstool grow.

TEACHER: That's sort of complex. Let's stick with our one plant.

JIM: How about grass? It's common enough and the whole lawn can be thought of as a culture.

TEACHER: OK, let's go with grass. Analyze it a bit. How does it grow? What does it look like?

JIM: Well, it's green, has pointed leaves. It's soft to walk on.

CARL: It has a root system that doesn't go into the ground very far—that can be torn up.

TEACHER: Let's see if we can turn our analysis of grass into a Compressed Conflict.

BETSY: Tender resilience.

DAVE: Silent compassion.

JIM: Soft spikes . . . or spears.

JON: Lushly erodable.

TEACHER: Let's take "tender resilience." How would you feel if you were a clump of "tenderly resilient" grass?

BETSY: Sensitive to wind that moves through you, yet you can spring back . . .

TEACHER: Let's get rid of the "you."

JIM: I feel hurt each time I bend down. It's more painful to get back up. I want to hide.

GAIL: Most of the time I feel good because I'm so green and healthy, but every now and then I think of my root system. It's not so strong that it can't be pulled up or washed away. I panic at the thought.

DAVE: Hey, wait a minute. Suppose it does get washed away by rain. The bare ground is exposed. How does the ground feel?

JIM: I would feel OK, so long as nothing bothered me . . . No I don't! I'm exposed! It was dark with the grass. Now that I'm out in the light I'll dry up and blow away or be washed away.

TEACHER: We started out with the question: "How was Socrates viewed by his culture?" We have been developing some metaphorical distance as a means of producing a fresh context for looking at the situation. What do our metaphors tell us about the question?

DAVE: Raw because it is exposed.

TEACHER: How did it get exposed?

BETSY: Socrates came along as a combination of heavy winds and violent rains . . .

JIM: . . . a relentless bastard . . .

BETSY: Shut up, Jim . . . and washed away the nice greenness of his society.

JON: Green like naïveté?

BETSY: Well, perhaps. At any rate, like Adam and Eve in the garden after being devastated by the apple. The Athenians saw their nakedness and felt guilty. More than that, they were angered—left bare, raw, exposed. It hurt.

DAVE: Tradition was pulled up by the roots, huh?

BETSY: Yes. And only Socrates didn't care about being exposed because it was his big idea. To rub it in further, he drank the hemlock and put Athens in such a fix it never recovered.

JIM: Huh? Why?

BETSY: Hey, look, stupid! The society was faulty, planned wrong.

JIM: Oh, bad five-year plan.

BETSY: Like trying to grow anything up a cliff, especially something with a shallow root system.

DAVE: Right. Like forgetting all about drainage systems or step-farming because it's easier just to throw the seeds and let them grow up any old where.

JIM: No. I think the Athenians did a little more planning than that with their society. It's just that underneath their affluence and splendor was only a little protective top soil, so to speak. It didn't take much of a storm to wash away, leaving all their elegant superficiality in mud puddles. Of course, they convicted Socrates of corruption! He exposed layer after layer of it. Athens wasn't such a green pasture after all.[23]

In this case the teacher used direct analogy, personal analogy, and compressed conflict with secondary-school students who were usually classified as unmotivated, to help them understand Athens and the trial of Socrates. Compressed conflict may not, however, be found in making the strange familiar because it can produce too much strain or distance on the issue at hand.

In making the familiar strange the emphasis is on creating distance in order to develop something new. The teaching process involves:

1. statement of the problem or task by the teacher;
2. use of analogies, particularly compressed conflict, in order to develop conceptual distance;
3. reconsidering the original task in relation to the analogies.

The following is an example of making the familiar strange.

BRIDGE-O-RAMA

You know what a bridge looks like. It is usually made of steel. It goes over a river or a highway or a railroad track. It is expensive and usually takes a long while to build. Is it possible to invent a new kind of bridge—a bridge no one ever thought of before? Well! They can't kill you for trying.

INVENTION PROBLEM: Invent a new kind of bridge that can be built quicker and cost less than present-day bridges. (Do not write until the 1st PHASE.)

FIRST PHASE OF INVENTION PROCESS: What insect bridges in some way? Don't limit yourself to thinking about insects that are themselves bridges. Maybe you can think of an insect that builds bridges. ("Inchworms.")

SECOND PHASE OF INVENTION PROCESS, PART A: Explain the mechanism(s) by which your example bridges. Be as detailed as possible. (He goes from small to big. He squeezes up and stretches out.

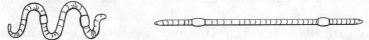

He looks like a slow-motion spring or one of those toys that goes down stairs—slinky.)

SECOND PHASE OF INVENTION PROCESS, PART B: Imagine that you are the insect you chose. How does it feel to be in the process of bridging? How do your muscles react? What are your thoughts? ("I've done it so much it's easy. I do it very slowly. The minute I get to the other side I pull the rest of me up with me. When my feet are on one side and my hands are on the other side I feel springy, so I hump up so as not to fall in.")

THIRD PHASE OF INVENTION PROCESS: Describe the fantastic way of bridging that would result if you built a bridge based on Part A and Part B of your 2nd PHASE. Don't worry about how crazy the result seems to be. ("It would be a stiff bridge with a hump or a soft bridge. A soft bridge would be crazier.")

FOURTH PHASE OF INVENTION PROCESS: See if you can force the fantastic into the possible; but don't lose the original quality of your fantasy bridge! Make your 3rd PHASE fantasy into a way of bridging that would actually work! ("I guess it would be a soft bridge—like elastic. It would give when cars and trucks drove over it. Maybe then they wouldn't break it down because it would give a little.")[24]

Here the process of making the familiar strange involves developing a unique idea through direct analogy, personal analogy, and compressed conflict.

The Teacher's Role

The teacher must be able to accept divergent thinking. There are no right answers in synectics, and the teacher should not channel thinking toward a predetermined solution. The teacher should also feel comfortable with the emotional and irrational elements of consciousness and be able to display these qualities in order to facilitate them in the student's work.

Applicability of the Model

This is a popular model because of its moderate structure and the number of synectics curriculum materials that are now available to the teacher. Synectics can also be used in most areas of the curriculum and is not limited to any single subject area or any particular age group. However, the synectics teaching process demands flexibility, imagination, and openness. The teacher must also develop skills in using the analogies.

The Learning Environment

Synectics is both instructional and nurturant in its learning environment. Through the use of metaphor it instructs the individual in creativity. This process nurtures the student's understanding of the academic discipline.

Figure 15

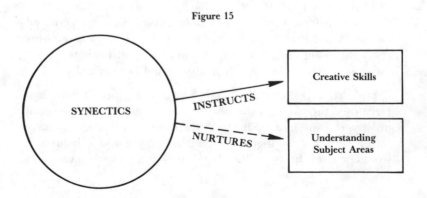

CONFLUENT EDUCATION

Theoretical Application

Originally introduced by George Brown and developed by teachers such as Gloria Castillo and Aaron Hillman, confluent education attempts to integrate the affective and cognitive elements in individual and group learning. The focus in confluent education is on consciousness integration. To facilitate this integration Gloria Castillo suggests that four elements are important in teaching.[25]

The cognitive domain represents intellectual functioning and knowledge. In using this model, Castillo identifies information that is stimulating and thinks of affective experiences that can expand understanding of the cognitive aspect:

> For example, while working on a math unit on geometric shapes, one of the goals is to have the children name and identify a triangle and a circle. An effective experience for primary children would be to have them "become" a triangle. I would ask, "How can you move? Where are your angles? Can you become a circle now? What do you have to do with your body to change it from a triangle to a circle? How can you move as a circle?"[26]

The affective domain contains the emotional aspect of learning and focuses on clarifying feelings, attitudes, and values. The

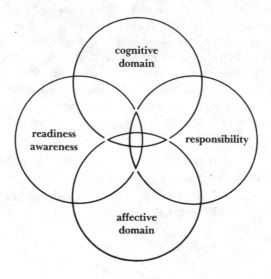

affective gives personal meaning to the cognitive domain; students can "live out" the cognitive through experience.

The readiness-awareness space represents what will be required when introducing new cognitive and affective concepts. The concept of readiness is familiar in the cognitive sphere and refers to such questions as "Does the student have sufficient vocabulary and knowledge to solve a particular problem?" In the affective domain it can refer to similar issues:

> For example, if I should want a child to respond physically to something that tastes bitter, he must first of all know how "bitter" tastes in relation to other tastes. He must have the vocabulary to understand what I want him to do. He must have skills to represent "bitter" in a symbolic manner, and he must have enough imagination to represent that taste by moving his body in a way that symbolizes bitter for him.[27]

This is an important concept in affective education since no strategy should be employed before the child is ready. Some of the techniques can be powerful, and if the student is not prepared, the technique will have no meaning or could even be harmful to him. An example of gradually increasing student readiness in the affective domain is outlined below:

> Initially, I must become aware of what each child is ready for, then take the necessary steps to allow him to be open to new experiences, both cognitively and affectively. Before having the child paint with his feet, for example, it might be necessary to do some preliminary work to get him to feel comfortable about removing his shoes in the classroom or allow himself to step into a pan of paint. This task might be handled by discussions of being and getting "messy," as well as by allowing him multiple opportunities to make a mess.[28]

Castillo says that the sphere of readiness-awareness also refers to the readiness of the *teacher*—her or his emotions, fears, and expectations as well as resource materials, information, and skills. The teacher should ask the question, "What do I have available?"

He must know how he responds to change, to each now, from second to second. He must know how he responds to confusion, to love, anger, joy, and grief. He must be aware of how he responds when he is threatened. He must be aware of his defense mechanisms and of when he is using them. It is necessary for him to become his own critic, for him to know when he is saying "I won't" rather than "I can't."[29]

The final area in the model is that of responsibility. This means that the student should eventually be responsible for his own learning and identity development. Of course the teacher does not abdicate control of the class. The aim is simply to develop the student's awareness about controlling his own behavior. The example in Chapter 2 of the sixth-grade teacher who developed two work groups shows how a situation can be created in which students are more responsible for their own learning.

The teacher attempts to keep these four areas in mind when teaching. He must first of all keep the student's level of readiness and awareness in mind. He then develops appropriate activities linking the cognitive and the affective in an integral way. Finally, he increases the amount of student responsibility in both domains.

Classroom Application

In her book *Left-Handed Teaching*, Castillo lists hundreds of confluent activities for the elementary classroom. The excerpt below is from her chapter on nature.

RAINY-DAY ACTIVITIES

Sprinkle different colors of powdered tempera on a piece of paper. Place it in the rain where it can be observed. Watch the rain paint a picture. Bring it in when you feel it is finished.

Concentrate on the sound of rain for a set period of time. Graph it, draw it, dance it.

Read "Chapter IX, in which Piglet is entirely surrounded by water," from *Winnie the Pooh*, by A. A. Milne.

Place a stick upright in a puddle. Observe it several times during the day. Watch the water rise or fall.

Watch a puddle grow. Measure around it with a piece of string. Measure it every fifteen minutes. Compare the length of string each time. (Each time a different child bundles up and "braves the storm" in order to measure it.)

When the rain stops, but while water is still running, have a contest floating paper boats down street gutters, rain drains, free-form ditches. Time the paper boats. Measure the distance they travel. Compute the speed at which they travel.

Watch raindrops sliding down the windowpanes. Time them with a stopwatch. Graph them. Imagine you are a raindrop. Write a story about your journey. Begin with "I am a raindrop."

Learn to read weather maps. Where else is it raining? What might the children be doing there?

Learn to read rain tables. Make your own and keep it up to date. Compare it with last year's data (available in local newspapers in your nearby library). Make predictions for next year.

Write words that describe the sound of rain. Write words that describe how you feel about rain. Use as many of those words as possible to make a poem or story about rain.

Work in groups to make a list of things that go up in the rain (e.g., rivers, umbrellas, earthworms). Be as creative as possible. Explain your list to another group.

Work in groups to make a list of things that go down in the rain (hairdos, flags, hillsides, etc.). Be as creative as possible. Explain your list to another group.[30]

This lesson moves from the cognitive to the affective in a very fluid way. Some of the cognitive skills involved are reading, writing, measuring, observing, graphing, and comparing. At the same time, the child is asked to be aware of his feelings and to use his imagination. Thus this is a confluent activity that integrates feelings and imagination with scientific activity. Castillo describes other confluent activities that relate subject areas such as social studies, language development, and mathematics to the affective domain.

An important element in the confluent model is being in touch with one's body. Not only are the cognitive and affective integrated in confluent education but exercises in sensory awareness and movement are used to relate body and mind. For example, the lesson below is presented in the unit on polarities.

POLARITIES OF YOUR BODY

Lie on the floor. Relax, close your eyes.

Become aware of your breathing. Begin to increase your inhaling and exhaling until you are breathing as deeply and as slowly as possible. How does the rest of your body feel? Now shorten your breathing until you begin to pant. How does the rest of your body feel? Now come to a place in between and rest. How do you feel?

Now become aware of the weight of your body. What parts are heavy? Where is the heaviest part of all? What parts are light? What is the lightest part of all?

Become aware of the temperature of your body. What parts of your body are warm? Where is the warmest place? What parts are cool? What is the coolest place?

Become aware of the texture of your body. What parts are rough? Where is it roughest? What parts are smooth? Where is it smoothest?

Imagine dividing yourself exactly down the middle. Compare the right side of your body to the left side. Take each part in turn and compare it with its opposite, taking time for each part.

Imagine dividing yourself at your waist. Compare the top half of your body to the bottom half in weight, temperature, texture, and other characteristics that come to you.

Compare what you know about the inside of your body with what you know about the outside of your body.

See if you can discover other polarities in or on your body. Take your time. When you are ready, open your eyes, sit up and join the group.

Talk about any surprises, anything you discovered that you were not expecting.

Now begin to walk around, paying particular attention to those parts of your body that surprised you, or the ones that are newly rediscovered. Be aware of your whole body.

Experiment with the parts you have rediscovered. Give them a voice, one at a time. What do they have to say to you and the rest of your body? Have each statement begin with "I".

"I am your left elbow. I am rough and hard and sharp."

"I am the base of your neck. I am tight and very warm."

"I am your bottom half. I give you support. I take you where you want to go. All you have to do is tell me and I will get you there."

"I am your top half. I make contact for you. I do all the thinking around here."

Throughout the day, continue to be aware of your whole body and all your separate parts. Pay particular attention to any messages you receive from any of the parts.[31]

The Castillo model also includes units on awareness of the here and now, sensory awareness, imagination, aggression, space, and art. Each unit facilitates consciousness expansion in a variety of ways.

The Teacher's Role

The teacher should be open and flexible in approach. Because the emphasis is on the here and now and on a fluid relationship between the cognitive and the affective, the teacher must be ready to move with each moment. Castillo gives a good example of this openness:

It has been my experience that with confluent lessons anything can and does happen. Sometimes I have chosen an activity that unexpectedly provoked so much laughter that I abandoned the goal of the lesson to explore laughter—what makes us laugh, what does laughter say, how can laughter help us to avoid our feelings, how does it show our feelings, etc. . . .

If I had taken the children's laughter as criticism of the planned lesson, something very different would have emerged. As it was, attending to the here and now, listening to the message of the laughter, and directly dealing with that message allowed me and the children a unique learning experience.[32]

Applicability of the Model

Because the emphasis is on fluidity between the cognitive and affective, these strategies tend to be unstructured and are thus appropriate for students operating at the moderate to high CL stages. The teacher must be able to maintain this fluidity and not emphasize one area over the other. Because of the skills demanded of the teacher, this model has not been so widely used as some others in this book. For the imaginative teacher, however, it offers rich potential for student development and growth.

Figure 16

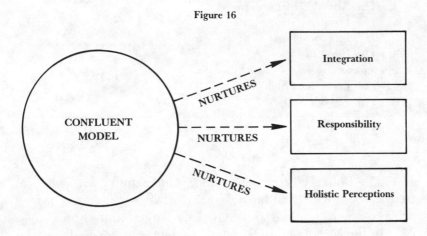

The Learning Environment

The confluent model is nurturant, since it tries to facilitate self-responsibility, holistic perception, and integration of the emotional, physical, and intellectual.

PSYCHOSYNTHESIS

Robert Assagioli, an Italian psychiatrist, is the founder of psychosynthesis. Although many of the methods in psychosynthesis are therapeutic in thrust, Assagioli acknowledges that the theory and many of the techniques can be applied to education settings. As an example, individuals associated with the Canadian Institute of Psychosynthesis in Montreal have been developing materials for the school curriculum. Most of the techniques try to facilitate realization of the Higher Self or a permanent center in one's being which is "above and unaffected by the flow of the mind stream or by bodily conditions"[33] and which can synthesize conflicting elements of consciousness into a functioning whole. conflicting elements of consciousness into a functioning whole.

Assacioli has diagramed human consciousness and the Higher Self as follows:[34]

1. The Lower Unconscious
2. The Middle Unconscious
3. The Higher Unconscious
   or Superconscious
4. The Field of Con-
   sciousness
5. The Conscious Self or "I"
6. The Higher Self
7. The Collective Uncon-
   scious

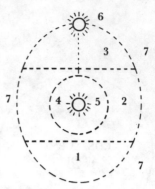

1. The Lower Unconscious contains elementary psychological activities, fundamental biological drives, and complexes charged with emotions, phobias and compulsive urges, and so on.

2. In the Middle Unconscious, experiences are assimilated and imaginative activities are developed before the individual enters waking consciousness.

3. From the Higher Unconscious, or Superconscious, individuals receive higher intuitions and inspirations—for example, artistic intuitions and altruistic love.

4. The Field of Consciousness represents our waking consciousness and the "incessant flow of sensations, images, thoughts, feelings, desires and impulses."[35]

5. The Conscious Self or "I" is similar to the Witness described in the section on meditation. It is the place in our consciousness where we can calmly observe the flow of thoughts and sensations associated with our field of consciousness.

The formal process of psychosynthesis involves four stages:

1. **Thorough knowledge of one's personality.**
2. **Control of its various elements.**
3. **Realization of one's true Self—the discovery or creation of a unifying center.**
4. **Psychosynthesis: the formation or reconstruction of the personality around the new center.**[36]

The first stage involves becoming aware of the first three regions of consciousness—of one's basic impulses as well as one's highest aspirations.

The second stage involves detaching or dis-identifying with the various aspects of the personality. The process of dis-identification allows the student to gradually gain control over his life instead of being "driven" by desires and impulses. Assagioli gives a brief description of the dis-identification process:

> Every time we "identify" ourselves with a weakness, a fault, a fear or any personal emotion or drive, we limit and paralyze ourselves. Every time we admit "I am discouraged" or "I am irritated," we become more and more dominated by depression or anger. We have accepted those limitations; we have ourselves put on our chains. If, instead, in the same situation we say, "A wave of discouragement is *trying* to submerge me" or "An impulse of anger is *attempting* to overpower me," the situation is very different.[37]

The third step involves expanding personal consciousness by following the thread that unites the lower and higher self. This is a difficult task and often involves taking on an ideal model.

> For some it may be the ideal of the artist who realizes and expresses himself as the creator of beautiful forms, who makes art the most vital interest and the animating principle of his existence, pouring into it all his best energies. For others it may be the ideal of the seeker after Truth, the philosopher, the scientist. For yet others it is a more limited and personal ideal, that of the good father or mother.[38]

An exercise in examining ideal models is included in the classroom application section. The ideal model serves as temporary link to the Higher Self.

The fourth step involves building the personality around the Higher Self, the unifying center. This is the actual psychosynthesis which contains several stages. First, the individual must develop an action plan. Some people follow a definite step-by-step formula, while others relate to their intuitions in a more spontaneous manner. An individual can use both approaches on the path of psychosynthesis. This will keep him from becoming too rigid, on the one hand, and from being too passive and negative, on the other. Once a plan has been determined, the individual then concentrates on utilization of available energies. This involves transmuting energy from unproductive activities to projects that are in harmony with the new conception of self.

Instances of such transformations have been observed and recognized by many people. When the Latin poet says, *Facit indignatio versus* (Indignation produces my poems), he shows that he has realized how an emotional wave of indignation, if denied a natural outlet through external action, can be transformed into poetic activity. Again, when Heine writes, *Aus meinen grossen Schmerzen mach' ich die kleinen Lieder* (Out of my great suffering I produce my little songs), he indicates that his pain has been sublimated into poetry, and thus transfigured into beauty.[39]

Next, the individual concentrates on developing aspects of the personality through different techniques and methods in psychosynthesis.

Finally there is coordination and subordination of the various energies and aspects of personality into an integrated consciousness. In this step the personality is reorganized around the Higher Self. Psychosynthesis, however, is an ongoing, dynamic process that involves conflict between different aspects of our being and a unifying center which tends to control, harmonize, and utilize these elements.

Classroom Application

To facilitate the psychosynthesis process, the teacher working with older or gifted adolescents could use the ideal model exercise, developed by Martha Crampton of the Canadian Institute of Psychosynthesis. This technique is useful in the second and third stages of psychosynthesis. The individual imagines different identities and eventually comes in contact with a model that can serve as a unifying center.

THE IDEAL MODEL

Introspection readily reveals the existence within ourselves of a multiplicity of semi-autonomous subpersonalities which come into play in response to differing circumstances and which are frequently in conflict with one another. These subpersonalities seem to be formed around models of behavior we have incorporated either consciously or—more often—unconsciously, and which are rarely explicit. Such models, which govern so much of our behavior, are generally not voluntarily chosen and tend to be derived from social conditioning. They lack the integrative value of models chosen consciously with participation of the inner self and our faculties of reason, creative intelligence, and will.

The purpose of this exercise is twofold. The first part is designed to help clarify and articulate the various and conflicting models which are determining our behavior at the present time. This prepares the ground for the use of the "ideal model" technique in which visualization is used to consciously choose and to begin to actualize a model of what we wish to become.

A. RECOGNITION OF FALSE MODELS

Select a place where you are comfortable and undisturbed. Sit in a relaxed position. Let your feelings become quiet. Clear your mind. Now consider the following types of conditioned and frequently unrecognized models which obscure our vision of what we are at present and what we can become.

1. We all have images of ourselves as less adequate in certain ways than we really are. Consider some of these ways in which you underrate and hence limit yourself. Think about it first, writing down any ideas which come to you. Then close your eyes and let images or pictures come into your mind which are related to the ways in which you underrate yourself. Study these images for a few minutes, learning as much as you can about them, noting the feelings they arouse in you, and reflecting on their meaning. Write down any insights you have had. (You may in addition, in this and the following steps of the exercise, use any of the other techniques for obtaining "answers from the unconscious" which you wish—e.g., visualization of the Wise Old Man or of words written on a blackboard; words spoken from a fountain or from the sky; spontaneous movement or drawing.)

2. Proceed as above to explore some of the models you have which are based on the way *you would like to appear to others,* on the ways you imagine other people would want you to be. There are probably different models involved here for the different relationships in your life—e.g., with a girlfriend, with a husband, with parents, with sisters or brothers, with your boss, with teachers, with various friends. Consider these relationships and how you try to appear as contrasted with the way you really are. Become aware of your feelings about these roles you play and whether the models they are based on help or hinder your own development. Be specific in trying to articulate and label the models involved. To help in doing this, you may ask yourself what underlying assumptions you are making in each situation about "desirable" behavior from the point of view of the impression you are trying to create. Remember to use the imagery techniques as well as conscious thought in working on this question. Record any insights.

3. There are also models more directly external in origin—models which other people project on us—ways they believe us to be or would like us to be which do not correspond to our inner reality. Proceed as above to explore some of these models, becoming aware of the feelings you have about their projections—those which you like and those you resent. To what extent do you allow the images and expectations of others to influence you or to become part of your own self-image?

B. Dis-identification from the False Models

Now let go of all these false, imposed models of yourself. Recognize them as roles you play or that others would like you to play, but which do not define the limits of your repertory. You may play these roles if you wish to do this, but you are not these roles and you can change them if you decide to do so. Let yourself become calm and centred again, taking whatever time you need. You may wish to take a short break in the exercise at this point in order to make a fresh start.

C. Choice of the Ideal Model

There are different types of "ideal models," some of a general nature which represent a fully integrated personality, and others of a more specific kind. The most practical type of ideal model to work with in the beginning is one which represents a particular quality or limited cluster of qualities—an underdeveloped psychological function, attitude, ability, or pattern of action which you would like to develop within yourself at this time. The true ideal model is to be distinguished from the various unrealistic, idealized models we sometimes hold which are unattainable and hence sterile. The true ideal model must be realistic; it is a vision or goal to inspire or magnetically "attract" us (and in that sense it is "ideal"), but it represents an *attainable* next step in our development.

Proceed as you did before, using both rational thought and the imagery techniques to choose an ideal model for this point in your development. Take some time to do this. Reflect on what you would like to become and what qualities would help you to do this. Let your thoughts and images come from that source deep within which is your Higher Self. Write down your insights and conclusions.

D. IDENTIFICATION WITH THE IDEAL MODEL: THE "AS IF" TECHNIQUE

The power of creative imagination can be used to help translate an image or goal into the concrete reality of everyday life. Having chosen an ideal model, visualize and imagine yourself in various situations in your real life acting as if you already possessed the quality, attitude or ability you have chosen to develop. See yourself as actually manifesting the thoughts, feelings, and actions that correspond to it. Practice in imagination your new attitude, using a variety of situations with different people and different circumstances. As every image tends to actualize itself in overt action, this is useful preparation for attempting to express these new attitudes in your real life. When you are visualizing yourself as having taken this next step, perceive your eyes, your expression, your posture, your gestures, your voice and your words as all embodying whatever that step represents. Feel what it is like to think and act in this way. If any changes in your ideal model suggest themselves as you do this, feel free to make whatever corrections or refinements seem desirable. The ideal model is not intended to be static, rigid, and confining. Rather it is flexible, dynamic, and capable of evolving in accordance with our own development and on the basis of the internal and external feedback we receive through experience in the world and inner prompting.[40]

Another technique that is useful, particularly at the fourth stage of psychosynthesis, is the use of imagery that can give the person a sense of personal integration and awakening consciousness. The following exercise, also developed by Martha Crampton, is a guided imagery exercise that can help a student visualize the process of spiritual development—an important aspect of psychosynthesis.

THE TEMPLE OF PEACE AND JOURNEY TO THE SUN: A GUIDED IMAGERY EXERCISE

<u>Objectives:</u>
—to establish contact with supraconscious energies: peace, warmth, light, etc., and with the transpersonal Self, of which the sun is a symbol. Some subjects relate more easily to the peace and silence, while others respond more to the sun.
—to bring these energies down to the personality level and to share them with the world.

—to establish the imaginal body of concentration on all the imaginal senses (first part). This makes the experience more vivid and meaningful. .

<u>Exercise:</u>   Visualize yourself standing at the foot of a mountain with a temple of peace on top of it. It can be any type of mountain at all and any type of temple. Don't try to force your imagery into a preconceived mold. If any of the suggestions I give you do not fit exactly what is happening for you, do not be disturbed. Simply allow your imagery to unfold in its own way, and follow the instructions as far as you are able to.

Allow yourself to become vividly aware of the space around you at the foot of this mountain. Notice the type of terrain. Is it barren or is it covered with vegetation? If there are trees or plants, notice what they look like. Go over to some of them and touch and smell them. (*pause*) Now take a good look at the ground under your feet. Is it smooth or bumpy? Are there rocks and boulders around? Is the earth bare, or is there a ground cover of moss or grass? Bend down and touch the ground. What does the earth feel like?

Now take a look at the path in front of you leading up the mountain. Is it wide or narrow? Is it steep or is it winding and gradual? Is it a path which has been traveled by others, or will you have to find your own path? Slowly begin to climb the mountain now, noticing all the sights, sounds, smells, and other sensations you may experience along the way. Feel the ground under your feet as you walk. Feel the touch of the wind or air on your face as you climb and the sun if it is shining. What kind of smells are there in the air? Take a deep breath of the fresh mountain air that surrounds you. Let yourself be filled with the joy and invigoration it brings. Notice how the scenery around begins to change as you climb higher and higher, and you can see further and further into the distance. Look around you on all sides and enjoy these expanding vistas. (*pause*)

Now imagine that time passes very quickly and you are already on the last stretch of your trip. The Temple of Peace is on the summit of the mountain not far ahead of you. As you approach the top, let yourself be increasingly filled with the spirit of peace. Now you have reached the summit and the temple is just in front of you. Look at it carefully. Approach it slowly and with reverence. If you are wearing shoes, remove them before entering the temple.

The temple has two different parts which we will visit. The first part we will enter is the Hall of Peace, and later we will visit the inner sanctuary. Now we are in the Hall of Peace. We will meditate here and allow ourselves to absorb the spirit of peace and silence which abides here. Let the peace and silence here fill each cell of your body. Let it permeate your heart and your mind. Drink deeply of the silence, and feel it wash away all your cares and agitation. Take whatever time you need to be completely filled with peace and silence. (*pause—2 minutes*) Know that you can return to this inner place of peace and silence whenever you wish. And now we will prepare ourselves to make our way to the inner sanctuary.

The "inner sanctum" of the temple is called the Sanctuary of the Sun because its roof is completely open to the sun. We will now enter the Sanctuary of the Sun with great reverence and aspiration to make contact with this high energy. As you enter the room, visualize a shaft of light coming down from the sun and connecting with you. Allow yourself to experience the flow of energy from this—the spiritual sun—into your whole being. Let yourself feel warmed, lighted, and energized by this contact. (*pause*) Realize that this shaft of invisible light is always with you, linking you with the Source and center of your being, your true Self, and providing a channel through which light, love, and spiritual power can flow into your personality and, through you, into the world.

Now we are going to imagine that you are being drawn upward on your shaft of light into the heart of the sun. Feel that all members of this group are making the journey with you on their own shaft of light and that you will come together again in the sun. You will be perfectly at ease and comfortable as you rise toward the sun; the temperature is neither too warm nor too cold. Feel as you rise that you are coming home—coming home to a place of great peace and joy and love where you really belong, where you can realize the best within you. (*pause*) Imagine now that your journey is almost over and that you have entered the boundary of the sun, along with the rest of the group. You all continue to move forward until you come to that place which is called the Heart of the Sun, that most sacred place in which the sun's light and energy is most concentrated. Feel that you will receive just the amount and quality of energy that you need at this time, and that you need not fear being overwhelmed by too much. As you approach the Heart of the Sun, be aware of the other group members who are there with you. Experience them as divine beings in search of their own light and try to meet them at this level. Feel a sense of companionship in your common search for this light. If there are any people in the group for whom you have had negative feelings, try to make contact here from center to center, so that you will be better able to work out any barriers between you.

Now imagine that in the very heart of the Heart of the Sun there is a most sacred place in which an eternal fount of wisdom resides. You may imagine this Source of Wisdom as a symbol of some sort—perhaps a very wise sage or an abstract symbol of your own. Just allow a symbol to appear in this sacred place and let this be the one you will have. Now approach this symbol with great reverence and feel yourself in living contact with it. If there is some important question in your mind to which you would like an answer, you may ask it now. Otherwise, just allow the symbol of wisdom to speak to you of its own accord; see what the inner voice wants to tell you today. If you feel the need to enter into dialogue with your oracle, you may do so. Continue to ask questions until you feel satisfied with the answer. Then remain silent while you absorb the meaning of this exchange. (*pause*) Whenever you feel ready, take leave of your symbol of inner wisdom, giving thanks for what you have received. Know that you can return here whenever you wish.

Now let yourself develop a yearning to return to earth again where you can utilize this energy and knowledge you have contacted in the sun, using it to transform your life. Whenever you feel ready, imagine that your sunbeam comes to take you back again. If you wish, you can imagine that it gathers you up gently into itself and that it helps you slide back down at a comfortable pace to the temple on the mountain. Feel the strong magnetic pull of the earth as you get closer to it and realize that the purpose of incarnation is to manifest the light of the Self through your life in the world. Feel that you are now approaching the Sanctuary of the Sun back in the temple on the mountain. See yourself there now with the other group members around you. Take a moment to feel your feet on solid ground again. Then look up and be aware of the shaft of light coming down from the sun which is still connected to you. Feel that you can maintain this contact with the beam of light as you go down the mountain into the world, and that whenever you need to, you can renew your contact with the Source of energy and inner guidance in the sun. Now we will begin making our way down the mountain again. Feel, as you do so, how you can utilize what you have received to make your life more beautiful, more real, and more radiant, how you can apply this in a practical way to transmute your personality and to serve the world.

When you reach the bottom of the mountain, imagine yourself standing in a gesture of blessing with the palms of your hands facing outward. Feel that you are sharing with others what you have received, by allowing the energy to flow forth from you in this way. You can make the gesture of benediction physically if you so desire. You may wish to send the energy to specific persons or groups or to the world at large.

Optional:

Now let us send forth mentally these thoughts together: "Love to all beings—North, South, East, West, Above, Below. Love to all beings. Joy to all beings—North, South, East, West, Above, Below. Joy to all beings. Compassion to all beings—North, South, East, West, Above, Below. Compassion to all beings. Peace to all beings—North, South, East, West, Above, Below. Peace to all beings."

Notes:

It is important to allow time after the exercise for sharing experience. Frequently people have profoundly moving experiences which they feel unable to share right away. If a few minutes are allowed following the exercise in which to write down significant insights, this helps to make a bridge to sharing.

It is helpful to introduce this exercise with a demonstration of the symbolic movements in a complete meditation cycle. This will make clear the various stages of centering and alignment, elevation, communion, descent, and radiation which are reflected in this guided imagery of the temple and the sun. Conversely, the visualization exercise may be used as an introduction to discussion of the stages of meditation. The stage of centering, alignment, or recollection can be said to correspond to the experience in the first chamber of the temple—the hall of peace or silence. There the scattered energies are gathered together; the physical and emotional aspects of ourselves are quieted so that they will not form an obstacle to contact with the transpersonal Self, and the mind is concentrated. The second stage in a complete act of meditation—that of aspiration or elevation, in which the consciousness is raised to the highest possible point—corresponds to the moment when, in leaving the hall of peace and approaching the Sanctuary of the Sun, the aspiration is raised to make contact with this high energy. It is continued in the ascent along the ray of light into the Heart of the Sun. The next stage—that of communion or reception of the higher energies—corresponds to the experience in the Heart of the Sun. This is the stage of meditation proper or contemplation, during which the mind is held steady in the light of the transpersonal Self and the intuition is activated. The following stage—that of descent—corresponds to the journey back from the sun and down the mountain. During this stage, the supraconscious energies are used to regenerate the personality and to improve one's life in the world. This is the stage of "grounding," in which it is necessary to discover a practical application for knowledge received and channels for manifesting our new consciousness. Finally comes the stage of blessing or radiation, in which the energy or insight received is shared with others. This is expressed on the inner planes by direct radiation of positive energy and on the outer planes by action and service in the world. It is important to emphasize the last two stages in the complete act of meditation, as these are most often neglected. Unless the supraconscious energies are integrated within the personality in a practical way, psychic imbalance can result, and unless they are shared with others, the Source will dry up or cease to manifest.[41]

Other exercises used in psychosynthesis are keeping a diary, techniques for developing the will, and auditory and imaginative evocation techniques. The teacher should gradually introduce a number of techniques, indicating to the students that some will be useful and others may not be appropriate for particular individuals. The task for teacher and students is to find techniques that are useful to the students in facilitating personal integration.

The Teacher's Role

This model demands a great deal from the teacher. First of all, he must understand the theory of psychosynthesis and have some training in the techniques. There are a variety of techniques available, and the teacher must choose the appropriate technique for the student. He must not merely "try out" the techniques but should be familiar with the strategies and integrate them into a developmental plan so that techniques gradually build on each other. Like the meditation teacher, the teacher of psychosynthesis should evidence centeredness and integration.

Applicability of the Model

The model is limited to teachers who are familiar with theory and have some practice in the methods. It is mainly relevant to

SUMMARY: CONSCIOUSNESS EXPANSION

	Meditation	Synectics	Confluent Education	Psychosynthesis
Aims	To increase awareness To develop a sense of centeredness	To increase creative and imaginative capacities To develop understanding of academic subject areas	To facilitate integration To develop holistic perception	To develop a sense of centeredness To use this center in integrating conflicting aspects of consciousness
Teaching Process	1. Explain meditation technique 2. Allow students to practice technique 3. Discuss meditation experience	Making the strange familiar 1. Information input 2. Use analogies to deepen understanding of the information or concept 3. Refocus on the information in light of the analogies Making the familiar strange 1. State the problem 2. Use analogies to develop conceptual distance 3. Reconsider the original task in relation to the analogies	1. Determine readiness-awareness level 2. Integrate cognitive and affective learning experiences 3. Increase student responsibility	1. Diagnose students' needs 2. Identify and present appropriate techniques to facilitate student integration 3. After using technique, open group discussion
Teacher's Role	Create relaxed climate for meditation	Create climate where creative and nonrational can flourish	Maintain fluid relationship between cognitive and affective	Match appropriate technique to student Evidence centeredness and create accepting climate for the exercises
Amount of Structure	Can vary, but usually high to moderate	Moderate	Low, with exercises in moderate range	Low with exercises in moderate range

adults and older adolescents (ages seventeen and eighteen) and to students in the moderate to high CL range. Although some exercises are moderately structured, the general process of psychosynthesis is fluid and moves the student to higher conceptual levels.

The Learning Environment

Psychosynthesis as a learning environment is basically nurturant, since the technique facilitates a sense of centeredness, regard for others, and integration of conflicting elements.

Figure 17

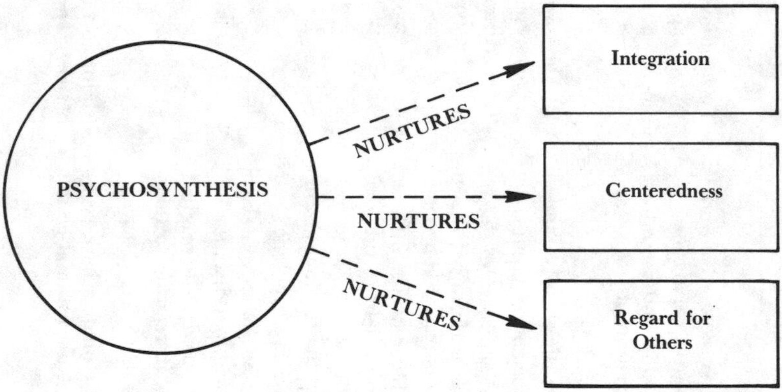

Notes

1. Robert Ornstein, *The Psychology of Consciousness* (New York: Viking Press, 1972), pp. 50–51.
2. Ibid., p. 68.
3. Robert Assagioli, *Psychosynthesis* (New York: Viking Press, 1971), pp. 217, 223.
4. Harold H. Bloomfield et al., "What Is Transcendental Meditation?" in *What Is Meditation?* edited by John White (Garden City, N.Y.: Doubleday Anchor Books, 1974), pp. 85–109.
5. Arnold Bruner, "Transcending Their Troubles," *Toronto Globe and Mail*, April 14, 1975, p. 8.
6. Ornstein, *The Psychology of Consciousness*, p. 107.
7. T. V. Lesh, "The Relationship Between Zen Meditation and the Development of Accurate Empathy." Unpublished doctoral dissertation, University of Oregon, 1969. The instructions for the meditation were adapted from this thesis, pp. 25–27.
8. Bloomfield et al., pp. 98–101.

9. Ornstein, *The Psychology of Consciousness*, p. 123.
10. Howard R. Lewis and Harold Streitfeld, *Growth Games* (New York: Bantam Books, 1972), p. 39.
11. Ornstein, *The Psychology of Consciousness*, pp. 128–29.
12. W. J. J. Gordon, *The Metaphorical Way of Learning and Knowing* (Cambridge, Mass.: Porpoise Books, 1966), p. 5.
13. Ibid.
14. Ibid.
15. Ibid., p. 6.
16. Ibid., p. 18.
17. Ibid., pp. 19–20.
18. Ibid., pp. 22–23.
19. Ibid., p. 23.
20. Ibid., p. 24.
21. Ibid., p. 25.
22. Ibid., p. 26.
23. Ibid., pp. 34–37. (Reprinted with permission.)
24. Ibid., pp. 144–46. (Reprinted with permission.)
25. Gloria Castillo, *Left-Handed Teaching* (New York: Praeger, 1974), p. 24.
26. Ibid., p. 26.
27. Ibid., pp. 30–31.
28. Ibid., pp. 31–32.
29. Ibid., p. 35.
30. Ibid., pp. 159–60.
31. Ibid., pp. 96–98.
32. Ibid., pp. 36–37.
33. Assagioli, *Psychosynthesis,* p. 19.
34. Ibid., p. 17.
35. Ibid., p. 18.
36. Ibid., p. 21.
37. Ibid., p. 22.
38. Ibid., p. 25.
39. Ibid., p. 28.
40. Martha Crampton, The Canadian Institute of Psychosynthesis, 3496 Avenue Marlowe, Montreal 260, Quebec. (Reprinted with permission.)
41. Ibid.

OTHER MODELS AND BIBLIOGRAPHY

Other Models

Creative Movement

Creative movement focuses on kinesthetic awareness or conscious perception of the body's movement and ability to "feel" movement. It is a method for consciousness integration through physical movement. Two texts available as introductions to movement are Geraldine Dimondstein, *Children Dance in the Classroom* (New York: Macmillan, 1971), and Joan Russell, *Creative Dance in the*

Primary School (New York: Praeger, 1968).

Biofeedback

Through the use of technology, the student learns methods of selfcontrol. He can learn to regulate states of consciousness, heart rate, as well as other aspects of his being. Limited in terms of applicability because of the need for biofeedback equipment. See Barbara Brown, *New Mind, New Body.* (New York: Harper & Row, 1975).

Hatha Yoga

Through various asanas or yogic postures the individual can become more centered. Hatha yoga is often done in conjunction with meditation practice. Several texts are available; a good introduction is Ronald Hutchinson, *Yoga: A Way of Life* (New York: Hamlyn, 1974).

Bibliography

Assagioli, Robert. *Psychosynthesis.* New York: Viking Press, 1971. A comprehensive overview of the theory and practice of psychosynthesis. A therapeutic focus, but some of the techniques are relevant to education.

Brown, George. *Human Teaching for Human Learning.* New York: Viking Press, 1971. An introduction to confluent education with many practical classroom examples.

———. ed. *The Live Classroom.* New York: Viking Press, 1975. A collection of articles that focus on Gestalt and the theory and practice of confluent education.

Castillo, Gloria. *Left-Handed Teaching.* New York: Praeger, 1974. Presents a model of teaching in confluent education along with a variety of classroom units. Most of the examples are for the elementary level.

Gordon, W. J. J. *Synectics.* New York: Harper & Row, 1961. Presents the theory of synectics with application to industrial organizations.

———. *The Metaphorical Way of Learning and Knowing.* Cambridge, Mass.: Porpoise Books, 1966. Applies synectics to education, with many examples from different subject areas and learning situations.

LeShan, Lawrence. *How to Meditate: A Guide to Self-Discovery.* Boston: Little, Brown, 1974. An excellent introduction to meditation. Approaches are divided into "structured" and "unstructured" meditation techniques.

Ornstein, Robert. *The Psychology of Consciousness.* New York: Viking Press, 1972. An excellent overview of research and theory on human consciousness. There is also a thorough discussion of meditation in relation to this research.

White, John, ed. *What Is Meditation?* Garden City, N.Y.: Doubleday Anchor Books, 1974. A collection of articles that present different views on the theory and practice of meditation.

CHAPTER 7
USING THE MODELS

The models of teaching in this book can be used in a variety of ways. First of all, they can help the teacher determine instructional and curricular objectives. Since each approach is linked to direct and indirect outcomes, the different models can clarify the teacher's expectations about a particular approach. If the teacher is using the moral development model, for example, he should not expect rapid change but only the most gradual development through the stages.

The teacher may have been using one of the approaches (e.g., classroom meeting) mentioned in this book without being aware of the specific model. In this case the model may help the teacher clarify his thinking about the approach and may suggest more specific instructional strategies. The teacher should see the approaches not as recipes to which he must adhere, but as beginning points in curriculum development—as conceptual springboards to alternative educational environments.

In terms of curriculum and instructional organization, several possible paths are open to the teacher. One is to identify an area of focus—consciousness expansion or sensitivity and group orientation—and work through the various models within that orientation. For example, the teacher interested in facilitating a positive self-concept could identify the conceptual levels of the students and choose the appropriate models. For students at lower conceptual levels, he could start with values clarification and then gradually move to moderately structured models. Sometimes the more structured approaches are useful in introducing students at higher conceptual levels to a particular orientation. Once into the orientation, however, the environment should be congruent to the learner's level of development.

Another possibility is for the teacher to identify the conceptual levels of the students and use approaches from different orientations to facilitate personal integration. For example, in working with students who are at moderate conceptual levels the teacher could use Erikson's model of ego development, role playing, the sensitivity-consideration model, and synectics. In teaching students at higher conceptual levels, psychosynthesis, psychological education, self-directed model, and human relations training would be appropriate. Table 5 lists the models and the amount of structure associated with each model.

Finally, some models can be used to plan and integrate the entire curriculum. For example, approaches such as identity education can be used as models for broad curriculum planning. Confluent education is an approach based on a curriculum-development process and is less structured in sequence. Instead there is constant movement between the cognitive and affective. Because the confluent teacher is constantly in touch with analytical aspects of the curriculum, this approach could also be used to plan the entire program.

Merrill Harmin, Howard Kirschenbaum, and Sidney Simon have outlined a model that could be used to develop curriculum in a manner that relates cognitive skills to values education. Their model is simple and consists of three levels: facts, concepts, and values. Each area of the curriculum can be broken down into these segments. A lesson in painting illustrates the procedure:

FACTS LEVEL
1. Stretch a canvas.
2. Demonstrate how to use a palette knife.
3. Name three warm colors.
4. What is a landscape?

CONCEPTS LEVEL
1. What is the function of perspective? How is perspective created?
2. Try to paint the still life you see before you.
3. Demonstrate how light and shadow are used in painting.

Table 5

Model	Amount of Structure	Appropriate Conceptual Level
1. Ego development (Erikson)	Can vary, but generally moderate	Moderate
2. Psychological model (Mosher-Sprinthall)	Moderate to low	Moderate to high
3. Psychosocial model (Hoffman-Ryan)	High to moderate	Low to moderate
4. Moral development model (Kohlberg)	Can vary, but generally moderate	Moderate
5. Values clarification (Simon & others)	High	Low
6. Identity education (Weinstein-Fantini)	Moderate	Moderate
7. Classroom meeting model (Glasser)	Moderate	Moderate
8. Role-playing model (Shaftel & Shaftel)	Moderate	Moderate
9. Self-directed model (Rogers)	Low	High
10. Communications model (Carkhuff)	High	Low
11. Sensitivity-consideration model (McPhail)	Moderate	Moderate
12. Transactional analysis (Harris, Berne, Ernst)	Moderate to low	Moderate to high
13. Human relations training (NTL)	Low with moderately structured exercises	Moderate to high
14. Meditation (Ornstein)	Can vary, but generally high	Low to moderate
15. Synectics (Gordon)	Moderate	Moderate
16. Confluent education (Castillo)	Low with moderately structured exercises	Moderate to high
17. Psychosynthesis (Assagioli)	Low with moderately structured exercises	Moderate to high

VALUES LEVEL
1. What would you like to paint if you could? What would you most like to communicate through painting?
2. What are your favorite colors?
3. Which would you rather paint? Rank the following from most desirable to least desirable. Then share the reasons for your order.
   a. a portrait
   b. an abstract
   c. a still life
   d. a figure
   e. a landscape[1]

This approach shows the teacher how value questions can be related to most segments of the curriculum. Harmin and his colleagues outline lesson plans for the following areas: literature, vocabulary, grammar, civics, history, social studies, mathematics, earth science, biology, chemistry, physics, foreign languages, home economics, physical education, health, music, religion, bookkeeping and typing, and shorthand.

There are other approaches that could also be viewed as curriculum-development models for the entire program. Glasser suggests that the classroom meeting model can lose its special status and become the basic instructional mechanism. Through the classroom meeting, the teacher can diagnose where the students are and design instructional strategies to meet their concerns. It is also a mechanism for dealing with behavioral problems and exploring interests related to the curriculum. Finally, even if a teacher is dealing with basic skills such as reading, the nonjudgmental atmosphere of the meeting approach can apply so that the student does not become anxious and tense.

Rogers' self-directed model has also been used as a starting point for planning "free" schools. The total school environment is designed so that it is conducive to self-direction and personal development.

Finally, Erikson's ego-development model is sufficiently broad in scope to be an agent for curriculum planning. If it is related to other complementary developmental models such as those of Piaget and Kohlberg, it can offer a number of criteria for designing educational environments—for example, teacher empathy,

confronting conflict, role experimentation, and the active process. I have articulated these criteria more fully in other con-
texts.[2]

Evaluation

Evaluating the effects of teaching models presents a difficult
task. A few of the models such as the Carkhuff and Kohlberg
approaches have evaluation instruments associated with their
use, but a great deal of training is required before they can be
implemented by the teacher. Most of the models rely on the
intuition and observation of the teacher and feedback from the
students to assess their usefulness. There are also some standard-
ized measures to assess such factors as self-concept. However, the
reliability and validity of these measures have been questioned.
Perhaps their principal value is diagnostic: that is, they could
help the teacher to assess student concerns and self-perception
and could indicate what teaching models are appropriate. A
number of these tests are listed in Hoffman and Ryan's *Social
Studies and the Child's Expanding Self.* Diagnostic techniques such as
"Faraway Island," described in the identity education model,
can also be useful to the teacher.

It is also possible to involve students in the evaluation process.
This can lead to shared expectations between the students and
teacher concerning curriculum outcomes. For example, the
teacher and students could develop a set of questions that could
be used to evaluate the students' development. Questions that
students and teacher could examine together might include:

Can I function effectively in a group?

Do I hinder or facilitate the group process?

Do I give and openly receive feedback?

Do I make personal value decisions and do I commit myself to
those decisions?

Do I support other students' efforts to make responsible decisions?

Am I able to communicate empathy, regard, and genuineness?

In what ways am I moving toward becoming a fully functioning person? In what ways am I not?

Am I becoming more centered and calm?

Am I developing my Higher Self? How?

Am I dis-identifying from personality models that are restrictive to my development?

In what ways am I more creative and imaginative? In what areas can I improve my imagination and creativity?

What values are central to my sense of self? Do I act consistently on those values? What values would I like to develop and realize?

What are my principal concerns? How do these concerns relate to my sense of identity? In what ways can I deal with these concerns in order to realize a positive identity?

Am I living in the here and now? Am I able to relate my thoughts to my feelings? Do I see things holistically or in segments?

Am I committed to growth and development? Am I willing to take risks or do I avoid opportunities for growth? Do I facilitate another person's growth and development? If so, how? If not, why not?

The final list of questions would depend on the models used in the classroom.

A Humanistic School

Models of teaching in affective education can be most effective in a school with a supportive environment. What are the elements of such an environment? First, a small-sized school is more facilitative of personal growth. Research shows that students in small schools assume more responsibility for their own development and the school's program than students in the larger school. Studies of schools in Minnesota, for example, suggest that secondary schools that graduated between 38 and 175 students per year were the least bureaucratic in atmosphere and also the most economcical.[3] Douglas Heath suggests several reasons why a smaller setting is more conducive to affective education:

> In a small school, a youth knows everyone whom he might eat with, meet coming to school, or play with. He knows when a stranger enters the school. In such a school, every teacher knows something about whoever is discussed in faculty meetings. The school's small size makes it a conscious act to ignore a student. Its large size makes it a conscious act to know one. I don't be-

lieve teachers realize how importantly the structure of a school affects their perceptions of students. A small school makes it possible to consider a youngster as an individual and not just one of 150 faces seen in classes each day. Teachers do not have to be so specialized; they can teach several different courses to the same students and so understand them in a broader context than is possible otherwise. Obviously, in a small school, teachers and students can participate readily in each other's lives, in decision making, and in the formation of expectations and the management of discipline.[4]

Another supportive element in implementing affective education is a school and a school system with stated aims that include personal integration. If personal integration is not a stated purpose of the organization, then the teacher would have difficulty in using the models. If he wants to be successful in using the different approaches, he may have to work with other teachers and administrators at developing a climate in which personal integration becomes an acceptable aim. Teachers should consciously build a climate where affective education is integrated into the curriculum. A group of teachers interested in affective education could meet on a regular basis to discuss their common concerns, sharing thoughts and feedback on a particular model of teaching. Sometimes discussing a particular student can also be a worthwhile experience, leading to ways in which the teachers can work cooperatively to deal with the student's problems and identify teaching models that relate to those problems.

Such teaching models as human relations training and transactional analysis can also be used to create a climate in the school that is conducive to affective education. A staff that works cooperatively and gives and receives feedback is more likely to use the models effectively than a staff that is locked into games and crossed communications. Some of the models, such as psychological education, can be implemented only within a team-teaching framework, so that communication skills would be essential to facilitating student development. In general, then, the models of teaching are not limited to the classroom but can be used to shape the school and even the school system as an organizational unit. In his book *Freedom to Learn,* Rogers gives an example of how the intensive group experience was used throughout a school system.

Spatial arrangements in the school may also be important. Teachers involved in affective education should certainly be willing to move desks and chairs into a circle for a classroom meeting or out of the way for exercises in confluent education. Ideally the school should have a quiet space for meditation and guided imagery. Even a corner of a room could be established for this purpose. As a general rule the teacher should be open to different spatial arrangements in the classroom so that they can be changed in relation to the model of teaching being used.

Although it is important to view the school as an organizational unit whose explicit aims and hidden curriculum are openly examined and integrated, the teacher is the key to any program in affective education. The teacher must be committed to his own personal development. If he is not open to himself and to others, there is little possibility that students will move toward personal integration. Many of the approaches described in this text should not necessarily begin and end in the classroom. Meditation, psychosynthesis, human relations training, transactional analysis, and self-directed learning are a few of the models that can be integral to human functioning in a variety of settings. This point has been made earlier in the sections on the teacher's role; however, it cannot be repeated too often that the teacher should be consciously working on his own development. Through this work, he will facilitate the student's personal integration. As he becomes more centered within himself and more open to others around him, he will be creating a space or environment that releases these qualities in his students.

Notes

1. Merrill Harmin, Howard Kirschenbaum, and Sidney Simon, *Clarifying Values Through Subject Matter* (Minneapolis: Winston Press, 1973), pp. 89–90.
2. John P. Miller, "Schooling and Self-Alienation: A Conceptual View," *Journal of Educational Thought* 7 (1973): 105–20; and John P. Miller, *Pathways to Autonomy in Educational Settings,* a one-hour tape to be published by Audio Seminars in Education.
3. Douglas Heath, *Humanizing Schools: New Directions, New Decisions* (New York: Hayden, 1971), p. 127.
4. Ibid., p. 128.

BIBLIOGRAPHY

Graubard, Allen. *Free the Children: Radical Reform and the Free School Movement.* New York: Pantheon, 1972. An excellent overview of attempts to humanize schools through structural changes.

Heath, Douglas. *Humanizing Schools: New Directions, New Decisions.* New York: Hayden, 1971. Discusses student alienation and then proposes a specific blueprint for a community-centered school.

Silberman, Charles E. *Crisis in the Classroom.* New York: Random House, 1970. This well-known work details the problems of alienation and then describes a number of alternative and experimental schools.

INDEX